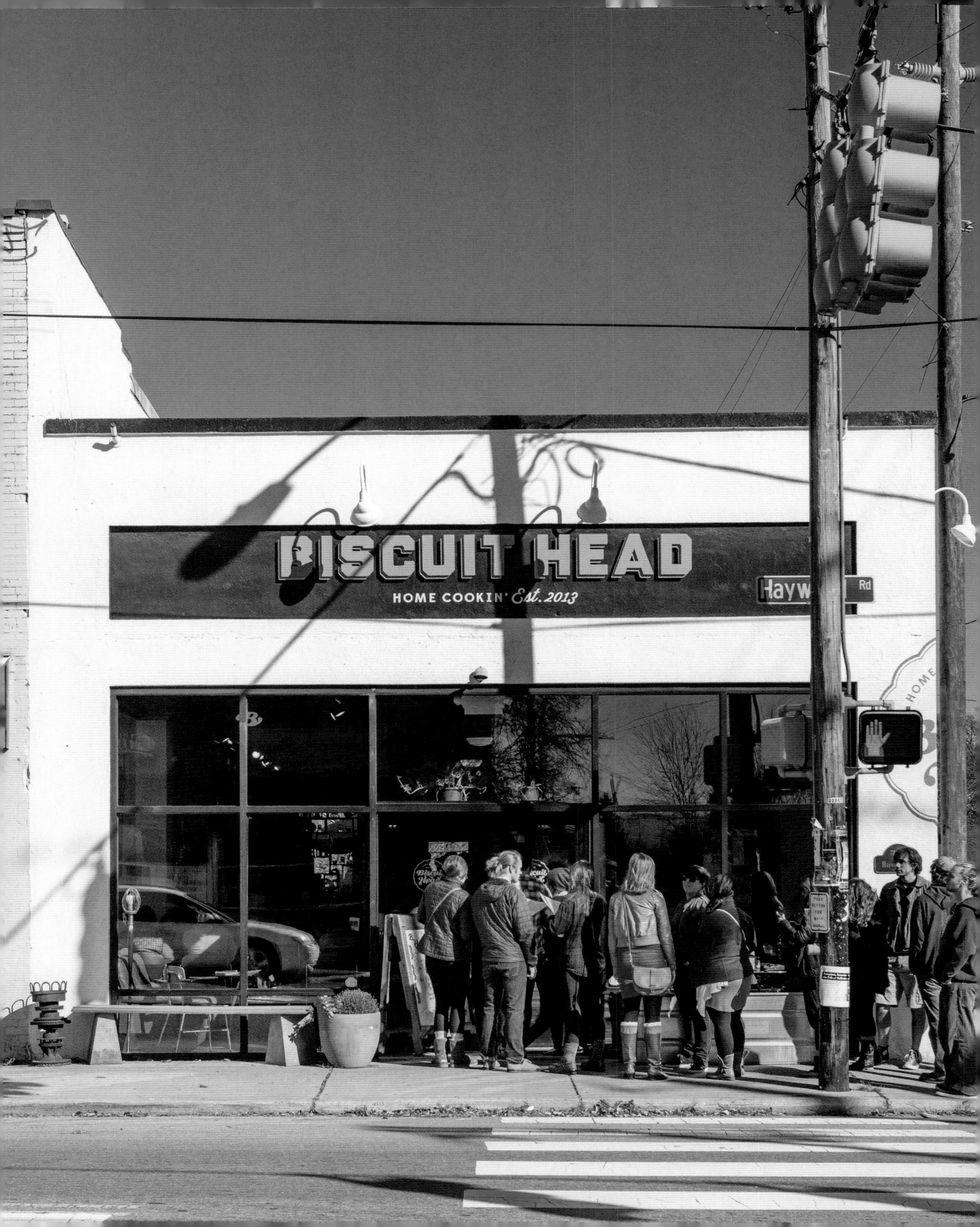
BISCUIT HEAD
HOME COOKIN' Est. 2013

JASON & CAROLYN ROY

Biscuit Head

NEW SOUTHERN BISCUITS, BREAKFASTS, AND BRUNCH

VOYAGEUR PRESS

Inspiring | Educating | Creating | Entertaining

Brimming with creative inspiration, how-to projects, and useful
information to enrich your everyday life, Quarto Knows is a favorite
destination for those pursuing their interests and passions. Visit our
site and dig deeper with our books into your area of interest:
Quarto Creates, Quarto Cooks, Quarto Homes, Quarto Lives,
Quarto Drives, Quarto Explores, Quarto Gifts, or Quarto Kids.

First published in 2016 by Voyageur Press, an imprint of The Quarto Group,
100 Cummings Center, Suite 265-D, Beverly, MA 01915, USA.
T (978) 282-9590 F (978) 283-2742 www.QuartoKnows.com

Voyageur Press itles are also available at discount for retail, wholesale, promotional, and bulk
purchase. For details, contact the Special Sales Manager by email at specialsales@quarto.com or
by mail at The Quarto Group, Attn: Special Sales Manager, 100 Cummings Center, Suite 265-D,
Beverly, MA 01915, USA.

10 9

ISBN: 978-0-7603-5045-4

Library of Congress Cataloging-in-Publication Data

Names: Roy, Jason, 1979- author. | Roy, Carolyn, 1981- author.
Title: Biscuit Head : new Southern biscuits, breakfasts, and brunch / Jason and Carolyn Roy.
Description: Minneapolis, MN : Voyageur Press an imprint of Quarto Publishing Group USA Inc.,
   [2016] | Includes index.
Identifiers: LCCN 2016014222 | ISBN 9780760350454 (hardcover)
Subjects: LCSH: Cooking, American--Southern style. | Biscuits. | Breakfasts.
   | Brunches. | LCGFT: Cookbooks.
Classification: LCC TX715.2.S68 R69 2016 | DDC 641.81/57--dc23
LC record available at https://lccn.loc.gov/2016014222

Acquiring Editor: Thom O'Hearn
Project Manager: Caitlin Fultz
Art Director: Cindy Samargia Laun
Book Design and Layout: Lauren Vajda
Photography: Tim Robinson

Printed in China

CONTENTS

Introduction   9

13   **Southern Pantry Must-Haves**
16   Pie Spice
16   Head Spice

Chapter 1: Biscuits   18

23   **All About Biscuits**
29   The Classic Cathead Biscuit
33   Gluten-Free Cathead Biscuit
34   Rye Biscuit
37   Mac 'n' Cheese Biscuit
38   Beet and Basil Biscuit
41   Roasted Corn and Jalapeño Biscuit
45   Beer City Biscuit

Chapter 2: On Your Biscuit   46

48   **Gravies**
51   Red Eye Gravy
52   Pork Sausage Gravy
53   Sweet Potato Coconut Gravy
54   **That's Our Jam (Bar)**
56   How to Can
59   Spiced Cherry Jam
60   Amaretto Marmalade
61   Raspberry Jam
62   Sweet Potato Chai Butter
63   Honeycrisp Apple Preserves
64   **Whip It Real Good (The Butter, That Is)**
66   Apricot White Ale Butter

67   Marcona Almond Butter
68   Sriracha Honey Butter
71   Raspberry Truffle Butter
72   **Infused Honeys**
74   Herb-Infused Orange Honey
75   Roasted Honey with Thyme
76   Chile Garlic Honey
78   **Hot Sauces**
80   Blueberry Jalapeño Hot Sauce
81   Strawberry Buffalo Sauce
82   D'Arbol Sauce

Chapter 3: In Your Biscuit   84

86   **Pimento Cheese**
88   Hoop and Jalapeño Pimento Cheese
90   Classic Pimento Cheese
91   Smokehouse Pimento Cheese
93   Mimosa Fried Chicken
97   Southern Fried Green Tomatoes with Chèvre Dressing
98   Chicken-Fried Tofu
101   Boiled Peanut Falafel with Peanut Butter Molasses
105   Fried Catfish with Tomato Sofrito and Fennel Slaw
109   Smoked Beef Brisket
113   Duck Confit Hash
117   **Bacon of the Day**
117   Makin' Bacon
118   S'mores Bacon
120   Blueberry Black Peppercorn Bacon
121   Habanero-Sorghum Bacon
122   Bacon-Wrapped Pork Loin with Smoked Maple Syrup

Chapter 4: On the Side   124

126   Biscuit Head Grits
131   Collards Callaloo
132   Sriracha Coleslaw
135   The Westers' White Bean Salad
136   Biscuit Head Mac 'n' Cheese
139   Southern Chow Chow
140   BBQ Pickled Onions
141   Corn Pudding
143   Okra Hush Puppies
144   Bacon Slab and Bourbon Baked Beans

Chapter 5: Eggs   148

153   Sunny-Side Up and Other Fried Eggs
154   The Sunny-Side
154   Fry 'Em Up
157   Perfectly Poached
158   Hollandaise Sauce
161   Scrambled, Please!
162   Quinoa Scramble
165   Oven-Baked Eggs with Biscuits,
      Gravy, and Chow Chow
166   The Perfect Quiche with Biscuit Crust
169   Kimchi and Bacon Frittata with
      Pickled Shrimp Salad
172   Red Beet Deviled Eggs
175   BLT Egg Salad

Chapter 6: Sweets   176

178   Biscuit French Toast
178   Sorghum Whipped Cream
178   Brown Sugar and Cinnamon Syrup
182   Biscuit Donut Holes with Lemon Curd
185   Lemon Curd
186   Quinoa Porridge with Pecan Sugar
188   Chocolate Biscuit Bread Pudding
189   Chocolate Gravy
190   Berry Biscuit Shortcake
192   Key Lime Pie in a Jar
192   Graham Cracker Crust
195   Buttermilk Ice Cream with Bourbon Figs
196   Bourbon Figs
199   Sorghum Seed Caramel "Corn" with
      Peanuts and Bacon
200   Buttermilk Pie

Acknowledgments   203

Index   204

About the Authors   208

INTRODUCTION

We're Jason and Carolyn Roy and we love biscuits. We also love Southern food, family traditions, the mountains of western North Carolina, and the city named Asheville that we call home.

While neither of us is native to our fair city, both of us come from families where food and the community it brings together are a big part of life. And lucky for us, we both had the crazy dream of opening a restaurant stuck in our heads before we met. Ever since we started dating, we've been working in restaurants. Between the two of us, we've worked just about every position front and back of house, and we've been part of many amazing restaurant families. At the end of the day, those families are what kept our dream alive.

Eventually, here in the beautiful, laid-back mountain town of Asheville, we decided to turn our dream into a reality. Our vision was this: a breakfast restaurant centered around Southern-style cathead biscuits. (These are just what they sound like—biscuits as big as a cat's head!) It might sound simple, but we believe cathead biscuits are magical. They are humble but delicious, and they are wonderfully versatile as the base for a menu.

We wanted our restaurant to be welcoming, fun, and lighthearted . . . just like us! We wanted it to draw on the community and be supplied as much as possible through local vendors. We wanted to treat our employees well and consider the environment too—composting and recycling whenever possible. It was also important for the restaurant to be a place where we could spread the gospel not only of biscuits, but of gravies, jams, and all other manner of delicious breakfast foods.

So we took the plunge. With the help of our friends and family, we tore down wallpaper, pressure washed, and painted. We moved heavy equipment (crushing a few fingers along the way). We laid tile, built tables, and constructed our jam bar—the idea for this came from salsa bars common in Mexican restaurants! Recipes were created and tested, and our staff was hired and trained. There were late nights and early mornings. There was laughter, arguments, and tears— nearly unbearable stress and unmatchable joy.

Then, on May 21, 2013, our doors were finally open. We knew it would be busy and we were prepared, but we still underestimated people's love and excitement for biscuits! That first week was crazy. We never anticipated having a line out the door, but we did. We ran out of food and found ourselves making trips to the store in the middle of the day. We arrived hours before opening and stayed long after closing to prep food and reorganize. We learned a very important lesson: no matter how prepared you try to be, some things just can't be tweaked until after you've opened the doors.

But we retooled what we needed to in the kitchen to meet demand, optimized the front of house little by little, and pretty soon the restaurant was running like a dream. If the line wasn't out the door, around the corner, and down the block, our employees started to think it was slow! Chaos became the new normal, and we all learned to thrive in it.

Over that first year we watched our dreams come to life, and it was more fulfilling than we could have imagined. We were so tickled every time someone was converted to the bacon of the day or had that aha! moment when they discovered we did gravy flights. In fact, we had so much fun and the restaurant was still so dang busy that we decided we had to do it again. With the help of our family and friends, notably the Westers, we opened our second Biscuit Head a year later, just a few miles across town.

As we write this book, we're just about ready to open our first location outside of Asheville in Greenville, South Carolina. And while there are no plans to keep building Biscuit Heads, you never know what the future holds! No matter what we decide to do, though, we will remain humble and true to our dream. Our very first customers, Fred and Justin, still stop by every week to eat and chat with the staff. We hope this book lives on in the same way and that you find yourself stopping by these pages over the years whenever you want a dang good breakfast.

Time to make the biscuits!

Jason and Carolyn Roy

SOUTHERN PANTRY
MUST-HAVES

In the South, our pantries are our secret weapons whenever it's time to create a great meal. Many people go beyond the basics, canning and preserving in season so that they have nature's bounty at their fingertips year round. (On page 56, you can find out more about canning if you choose to do the same.) In this section, we'll help you fill your pantry with some of our favorite staples and make sure you have everything you need to make the recipes in this book—and beyond. If it takes a little work to find a few of the more obscure ingredients, embrace the trip to a new store or the visit to a new website! Remember that the journey to finding a new food is often half the fun.

Flours

All-purpose flour or AP flour: This is just regular old flour—you probably already have some in your pantry! It is one of two flours we blend to make our biscuits. We use White Lily brand.

Cake flour: Cake flour, in general, is a softer and lighter-grained flour milled from soft winter wheat, and you need it to make angel-soft and cloud-like biscuits, cakes, and pastries. We prefer King Arthur. Keeping cake flour on hand is essential to the perfect flour blend for just about all our biscuits. (Except gluten-free, of course!)

Gluten-free (GF) flour mix: We have tried lots of different GF flours and have experimented with making our own mixes and blends, but Bob's Red Mill makes the best. Make it easy on yourself and try this out for just about all of your GF baking needs.

Grains, Seeds, and Legumes

Cornmeal: Yellow or white, fine-ground or coarse—for many recipes, it will be your choice. Still, no matter your favorite, once you cook with cornmeal, we think you'll agree that it's nice to always have it on hand. There are so many different things you can do with it, from making cornbread or our Roasted Corn and Jalapeño Biscuit (page 41) to making hush puppies or using it as a breading on foods.

Grits (white or yellow): Come on, this is a Southern pantry! You better have some good grits in there and learn how to cook them. We love to use stone-ground and coarse grits. They take longer to cook, but once you take a bite, you know they are worth all the effort.

Steel-cut oats: For breakfast people, oats are a staple. Steel-cut oats are so healthy, and you can make good old-fashioned oatmeal, a nice porridge, or cookies with them—you can even use them as a coating for other foods. We usually get ours in the bulk section and keep a nice big container of them on hand.

Quinoa: Quinoa is one of our favorite things to cook and eat. It is so incredibly good for you and packed with protein. Get whichever kind you like best—rainbow, red, white—they're all amazing. We often cook it in the rice cooker, which is so simple. Try keeping a container of cooked quinoa in the fridge and add it to scrambles, salads, stir-fries, or whatever you want for added texture and nutrition.

Whole-grain barley: We love to have an assortment of healthy grains on hand, and along with quinoa, this is another favorite. Adding barley to your biscuits and other baked goods adds a beautiful little pop of texture and tons of health benefits. We grab this one in the bulk section at the grocery store as well.

Sorghum seeds: Sorghum seeds are amazing popped and eaten like popcorn (see page 199), but the grain is also delicious when cooked traditionally. It can be used in place of rice or couscous in your meals. There really are so many ways to use sorghum, so experiment. If you can't find sorghum seeds in your local grocery store, you can order them online from www.nuts.com.

Dried beans: Navy beans, lima beans, red beans, and black-eyed peas are some of our favorites to have on hand. We make all kinds of things with them, from soups to baked beans to unique spins on hummus.

Nuts: We always have a variety of nuts in the pantry to use for baking, cooking, and eating as a healthy snack. Pecans, walnuts, peanuts, and many others are actually grown in the South, so we love to try to find local nuts whenever possible.

Baking

White sugar: This is the straight-up granulated white sugar you grew up on. Oftentimes you need its no-frills sweetening power.

Brown sugar: Brown sugar is sugar with molasses added to it. There are two different types, light and dark. The dark sugar has more molasses added to it, giving it a darker color and a more robust flavor. We lean toward using light brown sugar so we can control the strength of the molasses flavor, but feel free to experiment in your recipes—especially if you love molasses.

Powdered sugar: This is white sugar that has been pulverized into a fine, snow-like powder. It's essential for sprinkling over some desserts, like the Biscuit Donut Holes on page 182.

Molasses: Molasses is the thick, sweet liquid that is produced when sugar cane is refined into crystal sugar. Blackstrap molasses is our favorite because it has the richest flavor. It is also the thickest molasses and the darkest in color.

Sorghum syrup: Sorghum syrup, like molasses, is a thick, sweet liquid, but it's produced from the juice of the sorghum stalk. The large grass stalks are run through a mill, and the juice that is collected from the crushed plant is cooked over an open fire and reduced to a thick syrup. We think it's so good on top of a hot biscuit! If you need to order sorghum syrup, try these guys over in Tennessee: www.muddypondsorghum.com.

Maple syrup: OK, so maple syrup isn't all that Southern—but we love it all the same. Maple syrup is sap that is collected from maple trees and boiled over a fire until it's been reduced into a sweet and delicious syrup. There are different grades for the syrup, and we tend to go for the grade A, dark amber variety from Vermont.

Honey: We recommend keeping at least three varietals of honey on hand as they can lend such different flavors to recipes. There are hundreds to choose from, but the best place to start is your local farmers' market. To get you started, clover is a good, neutral honey. But please seek out some local varietals where you live. Once you taste a few unique honeys, you'll be in love!

We also recommend keeping the following items in your pantry: **vanilla extract, almond extract, baking powder, baking soda, unsweetened cocoa powder, graham crackers, and dried fruits (such as figs, cherries, and apricots).**

Spices and Seasonings

We love spices at Biscuit Head, and fresh spices are the best. You can tell you're unlocking big and bold flavors when you grind them yourself too. We highly recommend buying whole spices whenever possible and using a spice grinder, pepper mill, or Microplane, depending on the spice. And of course, fresh is best. Don't store your spices forever!

Here is a short list of spice must-haves: **coriander seed, cumin seed, whole clove, whole nutmeg, cinnamon sticks, mustard seeds, smoked paprika, kosher salt, and whole black peppercorns.**

We also like to make a couple of different spice blends that are very versatile and useful in everyday cooking. We mix up a big batch and keep them in Mason jars in the pantry.

PIE SPICE

This is an easy and versatile spice to add to a dish when it needs that perfect fall flavor. Try it in coffee too! We recommend grinding your own spices, but preground will work as well. To grind spices you can use a spice grinder or a Microplane.

Ingredients

¼ cup ground cinnamon

1 tablespoon ground nutmeg

1 tablespoon ground dried ginger

1 tablespoon ground allspice

1 teaspoon ground clove

1 teaspoon ground cardamom

1 teaspoon ground dried lemon peel

Add all the spices to an airtight container and shake to combine. Store for up to a year.

HEAD SPICE

This is an all-purpose seasoning that we use at the restaurant and at home. It's great for seasoning meats, potatoes, and all sorts of other things.

Ingredients

¾ cup kosher salt

1 ½ tablespoons smoked paprika

1 ½ tablespoons garlic powder

1 ½ tablespoons freshly cracked black pepper

½ tablespoon dried mustard

½ tablespoon chili powder

¼ tablespoon ground coriander

¼ tablespoon ground cumin

¼ tablespoon cayenne powder

½ teaspoon red pepper flakes

¼ teaspoon curry powder

Add all the spices to an airtight container and shake to combine. Store for up to a year.

Top-Secret Stuff

OK, maybe the ingredients that follow are not actually top secret. But they are a few pantry items we're mighty fond of and that you should probably keep on hand as well.

Bacon fat: When you make bacon, drain off the fat into a Mason jar instead of throwing it away. Store the Mason jar in the fridge and bust out the bacon fat to fry just about anything that could use a flavor boost.

Other frying oils: Man cannot live on bacon grease alone. Vegetable oil is our go-to for neutral frying in this book, but we also love lard and peanut oil, depending on the recipe. Some folks are allergic to peanuts, and vegetarians don't like their food to be fried in lard, so make sure to check with your guests if you use these fats.

Assortment of hot sauces: We can't live without our hot sauces, both homemade (page 78) and store-bought. Your selection is pretty much up to you, but it must include Frank's RedHot!

Duke's mayonnaise: Widely available and revered in the South, this mayonnaise is worth a special order if you've never tried it. The flavor is unique.

Jar of diced pimentos: Pimentos are simply cherry peppers that have been cooked and canned. They have a nice sweet flavor and are a staple in pimento cheese recipes (see page 86).

Whole-grain mustard: We like to keep spicy whole-grain mustard on hand to add a kick to some recipes and sandwiches. You'll find it's also useful for marinades, dressings, and all sorts of other things.

Assortment of pickles: Pickles are wonderful both as part of a before-meal appetizer and as an ingredient. Bonus if your pickles are homemade!

CHAPTER 1

★

Biscuits

As you might have guessed if you've visited our restaurant—or heck, by the title of this book—we think biscuits are just about the perfect food. Break a warm biscuit open, and you'll notice along with the steam out comes early biscuit memories. Maybe you grew up in the South and remember stopping by that tiny mom-and-pop biscuit shop on the way to school. You'd run in with your mom or dad and grab a biscuit to go most times, but once in a while you'd get to stay and enjoy the hustle and bustle of the restaurant as you ate a full country breakfast. Or maybe biscuits remind you of Sunday mornings, when you'd wake up to find mom and grandma covered in flour, rolling and cutting biscuits on the dining room table. It's also possible you didn't grow up in the "biscuit belt" and that your first memory of a biscuit comes from a Southern vacation. That doesn't make your biscuit memory any less special!

As for us, we're reminded of the time we spent carefully listening to our parents and learning the techniques friends and family had already mastered. Our love and respect for cooking grew from the cooks in our families and seeing happiness and satisfaction on their faces as the rest of the family tucked in. Nostalgia. Family. Tradition. Heritage. These are things that you can't taste but still leave you feeling full. And while both our families eat bagels, English muffins, and toast, our earliest food memories are inextricably tied to biscuits.

So biscuits make us feel all warm and fuzzy inside—you get it! However, from a culinary standpoint, biscuits are also quite special. Their smell can literally draw people in from the streets. Their dueling textures—the crunchy and brown exterior and the pillowy soft center—provide plenty of interest. And when their rich, buttery flavors are balanced perfectly with buttermilk and salt, they have a rare ability to complement nearly anything.

Tasty on their own, they shine when smothered in butter and jam or gravy. They can somehow make irresistible foods—crunchy fried chicken, sausage, or pimento cheese—even better. However, while you might think of biscuits as a breakfast food, they actually pair equally well with lunch and dinner and even dessert! In fact, to take it even further, biscuits not only play well with Southern food but with flavors from many countries and regions of the world. Think of biscuits as a delicious blank canvas and the perfect vehicle for exploring and marrying flavors. The possibilities and combinations are endless, which makes us love them even more. So join us! Let's make some biscuits!

ALL ABOUT BISCUITS

★ ★ ★

Ah, now we reach the part of the book where we can get philosophical: what is a biscuit? Well, we've found the biscuit can have many forms and variations with a range of textures, flavors, and appearances. The most common types these days seem to be the rolled-and-cut style of biscuit, which is leavened with baking powder, and the drop biscuit, which has a wetter dough that's scooped into the pan to be baked. Another type of biscuit familiar to many in the South is the angel biscuit, which uses yeast and requires extra time to rise before baking.

Scones, on the other hand, are biscuits that typically contain cream and require rolling but no raising. Biscotti are another common variation closely related to the original biscuit, though they are baked twice. This makes them dry and hard, which gives them a longer shelf life— perfect for the days before refrigeration when traveling short distances took a long time.

While all of these biscuits are delicious in their own right, the drop biscuit is our favorite. The style we make is also known as a cathead because of its size—it cooks up about as big as a cat's head! Some say the texture on top plays into the name as well; if you use your imagination, you can sometimes find shapes that resemble ears, a nose, and maybe even tufts of cat fur. In any case, these biscuits have the texture and flavor that we love and that we're now known for.

When baking them at home, you'll find there's a lot to love beyond the taste. They can be made quickly and baked on large sheet pans, which is helpful if you're feeding a crowd. You can easily change the size by adjusting to a larger or smaller scoop. You can easily adjust the baking time by changing both size and spacing (closer together equals longer baking times and farther apart equals shorter baking times). Another bonus feature of these biscuits, as you'll see, is their ability to be modified. You can add some Cheddar cheese, fresh herbs, or even brown sugar to change the flavor.

Play with Your Food

For us, cooking is fun, creative, and ever-changing. This means that we like to play with our food. (Shh! Don't tell mom.) Seriously, we use recipes as guidelines and ideas as starting points; we encourage you to do the same. Play with flavors to take a recipe of ours and make it yours. If you like spicy food and the recipe calls for one medium deseeded jalapeño, leave the seeds in or add an extra pepper or two. If the recipe calls for Cheddar cheese but your favorite cheese is Brie or Gruyère, swap it for one of those and see what happens!

Also, if you don't already, start cooking with your senses. Start paying attention to the colors, appearances, and smells as you prepare and cook food. If the recipe says to bake for 20 minutes but the tops aren't the golden brown you're looking for, bake them longer. You'll find that in no time you'll be learning the little things, from the way the tops of a muffin form a perfect little dome to the way a certain cake jiggles (or doesn't) when it's done. In short, learn the techniques and then change the details to suit your own preferences. Sometimes it might not work out or be the best thing you've made, but other times you may create something unexpected and delicious. For us, that is one of the most rewarding parts of cooking.

Deconstructing the Biscuit

Now that you know all about the different types of biscuits, it's important to know what exactly goes into one. Biscuits always comprise four main types of ingredients: fat, liquid, flour, and a leavening agent. (No, not like a double agent or biscuit spy—a leavening agent is what causes the biscuits to rise.) There is a bit of wiggle room among these categories, and people will swear by certain ingredients, claiming that they make for the best biscuit. While some may say you absolutely have to use White Lily flour or that a biscuit without lard is a tragedy not even bested by Shakespeare, if you have an understanding of what each ingredient does and what choices you have when baking your biscuits, you can eventually make your own rules.

Let's start with the **fat**. The most common fats used in biscuits are lard, butter, shortening, and margarine. Lard is a pure fat that comes from pigs—obviously not a good choice for vegetarians. (By pure fat, we mean it is all fat and thus has no liquids in it, unlike butter and margarine.) When using lard, you can expect your biscuits to be a bit dense but with a rich and unique flavor.

On the flip side, we've found the liquids and milk fats found in butter and margarine will create more steam inside the biscuit when they reach high enough temperatures, and that steam must find a way out. The steam creates tiny little passageways and tunnels throughout the dough in order to escape, creating a lighter, taller, and fluffier biscuit. Butter and margarine are also easier to cut into the flour, and they both provide a boost of buttery flavor—something we personally like a lot of in our biscuits. So, yes, as you might have guessed, we are on team butter!

The **liquid** is your next big decision, but it is a much less divisive choice. Most people use either milk or buttermilk. If you use milk, you will have a lighter, less complex flavor. With buttermilk, you'll get a rich creaminess and just a hint of that sour bite. Now, you might think that sourness is not something you want baked into your biscuit. However, think of the flavor when you add just a bit of sour cream to your mashed potatoes or when you use just a small amount in a cake. The sour note is very subtle and hard to pick out on its own, but it adds a soft complexity. Can you guess which one we prefer? (It's full-fat buttermilk for our biscuits!)

Flour is another ingredient that people feel quite strongly about. Here in the South, due to climate, most wheat farmers grow a red winter wheat that produces a softer and lower-protein flour. When you bake a biscuit or a cake with this type of flour, you really can tell the difference. You will end up with a softer, fluffier biscuit, which is exactly what we're looking for. We like to use a soft, low-protein flour like White Lily for half of the flour. If you can't find White Lily, you can also substitute another brand of all-purpose flour.

Note: White Lily has been our favorite flour not only because of the variety of wheat used, but also due to the fact that they mill it finer and process it differently than other flours on the market. There is a bit of Southern flour controversy looming around that particular brand these days because the wheat they use is no longer grown in the South, but they do still use the lower-protein red winter wheat.

The other half of our flour blend is another low-protein flour commonly known as cake flour. By combining the flours, we get a balance between structure and airiness, creating the perfect bite.

The **leavening agent** is the last component of the biscuit, and while it's not the star of the show, it is an equally important ingredient in the baking process. Remember that the fat and liquid steaming inside the dough helps to raise the biscuits and make them taller, but that steam can't do the job alone. If you make angel biscuits, you'll use yeast, but for pretty much every other variety of biscuit, bakers use a chemical leavening agent—most commonly, baking powder.

Making Biscuits

Now we are going to teach you how to combine these four main ingredients in a way that has traveled down family trees and through generations to create a batch of biscuits that is simply delicious. Our sample biscuit in this section will be our Classic Cathead Biscuit (page 29). Of course, we encourage you to experiment with some of the different varieties of biscuits and possible ingredients to come up with your own perfect biscuit as well. But let's walk before we run, so to speak.

You'll notice our biscuit recipe calls for more than one type of flour in order to achieve the flavor and texture that we want. When combining these flours, it's important to sift them together so that they're incorporated thoroughly and give you a consistent finished product. If you already have a sifter, go ahead and use that to mix your different types of flours and your baking powder. You can also use a wire mesh strainer. Just put all of the dry ingredients right into it, over a bowl, and gently tap it until all of the mixture has fallen through. Once completely sifted, your dry ingredients are ready for the butter.

The butter needs to be evenly distributed throughout the flour while remaining in small pieces. You do not want to cream or melt your butter like as would to make cookies, because that will prevent you from getting the flaky layers and height that you're looking for. It's helpful to have your butter as cold as possible for this step so it doesn't melt or overincorporate into the flour.

At the restaurant, we push the butter through a roasting pan rack, which produces small squares, and then we snap it into the flour. At home, you can do the same thing by cutting butter into small cubes with a sharp knife and then snapping it in.

Wait, what? Snap? Yep! The technique known as snapping is when you take the butter between your forefinger and thumb and make a snapping motion. This makes thin sheets or ribbons of butter that will fold into the dough perfectly and then rise in the oven in beautiful layers.

After the butter is snapped in and incorporated throughout, you will add the buttermilk and fold it in. It's important to not overmix your dough at this point. If you overmix, it will get too dense when you bake it. So fold it until it's just barely mixed together. In fact, it's fine to have a few dry spots.

Once the dough is mixed, you'll want to scoop it onto a greased baking sheet. We like to use a simple pan spray to avoid sticking and an ice cream scoop to evenly distribute it onto the sheet. The ice cream scoop makes the perfect dome shape and ensures that all of your biscuits will be the same size and bake together evenly. (Don't worry if you don't have an ice cream scoop handy—we have used a ladle to scoop out the biscuit dough and it is a fine substitute that will still form the nice dome shape you're looking for.) When spacing the biscuits on the pan, it's important to have them each just touching one another. This causes the biscuits to rise even higher!

These little beauties will be popped into your oven (preheated to 375°F) and then baked until they're done.

How do you know when they're done? We provide approximate bake times for each biscuit, but the best way to figure it out is by using your senses, of course! Our bake times are only a place to start because there are so many variables that can affect your biscuits. What kind of oven do you have—convection or regular? What size and shape biscuits did you make? Even the altitude of where you live can change how long it takes to bake something. We recommend setting a timer for 5 minutes shorter than the suggested times in this book and then checking them periodically after that. Once they are golden brown and firm to the touch, they're done!

One thing to keep in mind if you're unsure of your biscuit cook time is that you can always bake a batch longer when you discover it isn't done enough, but you can't unbake your biscuits! If they're overcooked and dry, that's how they will stay (well, unless they're smothered in gravy of course).

THE CLASSIC CATHEAD BISCUIT

Yield: 6 large (5-ounce) biscuits

This is our favorite biscuit recipe and the main recipe we use at Biscuit Head. In other words, if you walk in and order a biscuit, this is what you'll get! The "secret" recipe was learned over time from years of baking biscuits and tweaking the method and ratios to make it just right. For us, this cathead is pure perfection. We love the soft, pillowy center offset by the crunchy, golden exterior. Use it as a base for a piled-high biscuit sandwich or break off a piece to use as the perfect scoop for gravy or other goodies on your plate.

Ingredients

2½ cups all-purpose flour (we use White Lily brand)

2½ cups cake flour (we use King Arthur brand)

¾ teaspoon kosher salt

1 tablespoon baking powder

8 tablespoons (1 stick) butter, chilled and cubed

2 cups whole buttermilk

Note: Why do we blend in butter this way? Well, as the biscuit dough cooks and the butter melts inside the dough, steam is released from the fat in the butter. This steam, and the fat's ability to produce it, helps the biscuit dough rise and also gives the biscuit its signature flakiness, lightness, and moisture. If you skipped the intro to this section, turn back to page 25 for more.

Preheat your oven to 375°F, making sure you have one of the racks in the middle of the oven. Grease a baking sheet or cast-iron skillet (pan spray works fine).

In a large mixing bowl, combine both kinds of flour, the kosher salt, and the baking powder. We strongly recommend sifting the dry ingredients to combine them.

Snap in the butter (see Note at left).

Add the buttermilk and stir very gently to fold it in. Take care not to overmix! Scoop the dough into your pan or skillet, making sure to keep the dough scoops right next to each other on the pan. We use a large ice cream scoop whether we're at the restaurant or at home.

Bake the biscuits for 20 to 25 minutes, or until they are golden brown and fluffy.

RECIPE CONTINUES

THE CLASSIC CATHEAD BISCUIT
(CONTINUED)

Make It Your Own

Here are some ideas for modifying our basic cathead recipe:

★ Add 2 cups sharp Cheddar for cheese biscuits.

★ Add 2 cups cooked, mashed sweet potatoes, a pinch of Pie Spice (page 16), and 1 extra cup flour for sweet potato biscuits.

★ Add 12 cloves roasted garlic, chopped, and ¼ cup fresh chopped herbs (thyme, rosemary, basil— whatever you like) for garlic and herb biscuits.

★ Add ½ cup chopped country ham and 1 cup shredded Swiss cheese for country ham and cheese biscuits.

★ These are just a few ideas, but you really can add anything you want to the dough for extra flavor.

Pairing Ideas

This biscuit is built to be delicious with just about everything in this book, from the jams to the gravies to all the creative fixins', but we have a few combinations that have become favorites at the restaurant. One in particular, the Mimosa Fried Chicken Biscuit (shown on page 28) would have our diners up in arms if it ever went away!

To recreate it, you will also need to make the following recipes: Mimosa Fried Chicken (page 93), Sweet Potato Chai Butter (page 62), Sriracha Coleslaw (page 132), and the Perfectly Poached egg (page 157). The beauty of this biscuit is taking everyone's favorite—a plain ol' biscuit with fried chicken—and tweaking it just a bit to make it something special. The brine in the chicken makes it unbelievably tender and juicy, the Sweet Potato Chai Butter adds a touch of sweetness, and the sriracha in the slaw balances the flavors with the tiniest hint of spice.

Another fun idea for this biscuit when you're hosting brunch is to serve it with a flight of gravies or jams. (See the recipes starting on page 48 and page 54 for more information.) Just like going to a brewery and getting a little sample of different beers, a flight of gravies or jams ensures there's something for everyone to love.

GLUTEN-FREE CATHEAD BISCUIT

Yield: 6 large (5-ounce) biscuits

As you might expect, it took quite a bit of experimentation to develop our gluten-free biscuit. After playing around with different combinations of flours in different ratios to achieve the perfect texture, we came across Bob's Red Mill gluten-free flour blend. It's a readymade blend well-suited for biscuits and has since become a staple in our kitchen.

Ingredients

- 5 cups Bob's Red Mill Gluten Free All Purpose Flour
- ¾ teaspoon kosher salt
- 1 tablespoon baking powder
- 8 tablespoons (1 stick) butter, chilled and cubed
- 2 cups whole buttermilk

Preheat your oven to 375°F, making sure you have one of the racks in the middle of the oven. Grease a baking sheet or cast-iron skillet (pan spray works fine).

In a large mixing bowl, sift the flour, kosher salt, and the baking powder to combine. Snap in the butter (see page 26). Add the buttermilk and stir to fold it in very gently.

Using a large ice cream scoop, move the dough into your pan or skillet. Make sure to keep the scoops of dough right next to each other on the pan. (See the photo on page 27 for an example of how to space the biscuit dough.)

Bake the biscuits for 20 to 25 minutes, or until they are golden brown and fluffy. The gluten-free biscuits tend to be denser and a bit drier than ones made with traditional flour. Make sure to serve them when they're fresh out of the oven.

Pairing Ideas

This gluten-free biscuit pairs well with everything that the regular—AKA glutenous—cathead does. For an entirely gluten-free meal, we recommend the Smoked Beef Brisket (as pictured on page 111). All of the components of that one are naturally gluten-free and don't need any modifying. For gravies, check out our espresso-laced Red Eye Gravy (page 51) and our Sweet Potato Coconut Gravy (page 53). These are both incredible and have no gluten! Or, if you can handle a bit of gluten, go for the fried chicken biscuit combo described on page 30.

RYE BISCUIT

Yield: 6 large (5-ounce) biscuits

We came up with this as a special one day in the restaurant, but then we fell in love with it. You'll find it's a hearty and robust biscuit perfect for any brunch or dinner. It also looks a lot like a "normal" biscuit, which makes its unexpected, unique flavor a nice surprise for your guests. Its heartiness pairs wells with a variety of meats and cheeses.

Ingredients

FOR THE BISCUIT:

- 2 tablespoons caraway seeds
- 4 cups all-purpose flour (we use White Lily brand)
- 1 cup rye flour (we use Bob's Red Mill brand)
- ½ teaspoon kosher salt
- 1 tablespoon baking powder
- 8 tablespoons (1 stick) butter, chilled and cubed
- 2½ cups whole buttermilk
- 2 tablespoons honey (any kind)

FOR THE BRINE WASH:

- ½ tablespoon kosher salt
- ¼ cup hot water

Toast all the caraway seeds in a pan over high heat, moving the pan around constantly to keep the seeds rolling and moving over the bottom. Once the scent becomes overwhelming and the seeds get slightly darker, they are done. Remove the seeds from the pan. Reserve half for the biscuit tops.

Preheat your oven to 375°F, making sure you have one of the racks in the middle of the oven. Grease a baking sheet or cast-iron skillet (pan spray works fine).

Sift both kinds of flour, the kosher salt, and the baking powder in a large mixing bowl. Stir in half of the toasted caraway seeds.

Snap in the butter (see page 26). Add the buttermilk and honey and stir or fold it very gently. Try to get most of the dry flour spots incorporated, but if there are still a few, don't worry about them. Don't overmix!

Use a large ice cream scoop to move the dough into your pan or skillet. Make sure to keep the scoops of dough right next to each other in the pan. (See the photo on page 27 for an example of how to space the biscuit dough.)

Bake the biscuits for 20 to 25 minutes or until they are golden brown and fluffy. While they are baking, stir the brine wash ingredients together in a small bowl. Once the biscuits are done, brush the tops with the brine wash and sprinkle with the remaining caraway seeds.

Pairing Ideas

This is a biscuit that pairs well with many different flavors, but we recommend trying it with flavorful meats like smoked and cured salmon, corned beef, or duck confit. In fact, it's hard to beat this combination: top it with our Duck Confit Hash (page 113), one of our homemade Hot Sauces (page 78), and The Sunny Side egg (page 154).

OTHER FAVORITES:

- ★ **Jam:** Spiced Cherry Jam (page 59) or Sweet Potato Chai Butter (page 62)
- ★ **Honey:** Roasted Honey with Thyme (page 75)
- ★ **Gravy:** Red Eye Gravy (page 51) or Pork Sausage Gravy (page 52)

MAC 'N' CHEESE BISCUIT

Yield: 10 large (5-ounce) biscuits

What could be better than macaroni and cheese combined with a biscuit? Add some bacon into the mix, of course! You can count on everyone around the table being impressed with this outrageously delicious trifecta. For those of you who think it sounds crazy to put pasta in your biscuits, trust us and give it a try. You won't be sorry!

Ingredients

- 6 pieces bacon
- 3 cups all-purpose flour (we use White Lily brand)
- 3 cups cake flour (we use King Arthur brand)
- ¾ teaspoon kosher salt
- 1 tablespoon baking powder
- 6 tablespoons butter, chilled and cubed
- 2 cups leftover Biscuit Head Mac 'n' Cheese (page 136)
- 2 cups whole buttermilk
- 1 cup shredded Cheddar cheese

Cook the bacon in a skillet until crispy. Reserve the rendered fat and chop the bacon into pieces. Preheat your oven to 375°F, making sure you have one of the racks in the middle of the oven. Grease a large baking sheet (pan spray works fine).

Sift the flours, salt, and baking powder together into a large bowl.

Snap in the butter (see page 26) and stir in rendered bacon fat. Very gently fold in the bacon pieces, mac 'n' cheese, buttermilk, and Cheddar cheese. Be sure to incorporate the ingredients thoroughly, but be careful, as always, not to overmix the dough. Remember that a few dry spots of flour are OK and will cook out when baked.

Use a large ice cream scoop to move the dough onto the greased baking sheet. Make sure to keep the scoops of dough right next to each other on the pan. (See the photo on page 27 for an example of how to space the biscuit dough.)

Bake for 20 to 25 minutes or until golden brown and delicious.

Pairing Ideas

This biscuit will taste great topped with BBQ Pickled Onions (page 140), Smoked Beef Brisket (page 109), and some Strawberry Buffalo Sauce (page 81). The acid from the hot sauce and the onions will help to cut through the richness of the cheese and beef, and everything will be complemented perfectly by the smoky cheese.

OTHER FAVORITES:

- ★ **Jam:** Honeycrisp Apple Preserves (page 63)
- ★ **Honey:** Chile Garlic Honey (page 76)
- ★ **Gravy:** Pork Sausage Gravy (page 52)

BEET AND BASIL BISCUIT

Yield: 8 large (5-ounce) biscuits

This biscuit showcases the beauty and the flavor of beets and is a fun addition to any brunch spread. Sure, not everyone loves beets, but to us they are one of the most perfect vegetables. The sweet, earthy character of this humble root comes together with fresh basil for a big pop of garden-fresh flavor in this biscuit. The bold red color will be noticeable in the flecks of beet, and the dough itself turns a shade of pink.

Ingredients

- 2 medium-sized beets
- 3 tablespoons olive oil, divided
- Pinch of salt and pepper
- ¼ cup basil, chiffonade cut
- 2 cloves garlic, minced
- 1 teaspoon cracked black pepper
- 1¼ cups whole buttermilk
- 5 cups all-purpose flour (we use White Lily brand)
- ¾ teaspoon kosher salt
- 1 tablespoon baking powder
- 6 tablespoons butter, chilled and cubed

Cook the Beets

Preheat your oven to 375°F.

Wash the beets thoroughly, scrubbing off any dirt. Transfer the beets to a shallow roasting dish or pie pan and coat them with 1 tablespoon of olive oil and a sprinkle of salt and pepper.

Place the beets in the oven and roast for 30 to 45 minutes. The beets are done when they are fork-tender.

Transfer the hot beets to an ice bath to cool them down. At this point, the skin should be easy to remove by rubbing the beets with a kitchen towel or paper towels.

Note: If you use a kitchen towel, make sure it is a towel that you don't mind turning pink! Also you will be caught "red-handed" if you don't wear gloves while removing the skins.

Shred the beets through the large side of a box grater or in a food processor.

RECIPE CONTINUES

BEET AND BASIL BISCUIT (CONTINUED)

Make the Biscuits

Keep that oven set to 375°F, making sure you have one of the racks in the middle of the oven. Grease a baking sheet or cast-iron skillet (pan spray works fine).

In a large mixing bowl, combine the beets with the basil, remaining 2 tablespoons of olive oil, garlic, pepper, and buttermilk.

In another large bowl, sift together the flour, salt, and baking powder. Snap the butter into the flour mixture (see page 26).

Add the beet and buttermilk mixture to the flour and butter bowl; mix gently. Use a large ice cream scoop to transfer the dough into your pan or skillet. Make sure to keep the scoops of dough right next to each other on the pan. (See the photo on page 27 for an example of how to space the biscuit dough.)

Bake for 20 to 25 minutes (until you see golden pink peaks).

Pairing Ideas

We like this biscuit with a nice flavorful soft cheese like Brie or reblochon, a good local honey, basil (or a pesto), and a little Marcona Almond Butter (page 67). Alternately, a rich balsamic vinegar and goat cheese would go nicely with this biscuit along with some summer greens.

OTHER FAVORITES:

★ **Jam:** Amaretto Marmalade (page 60) or Honeycrisp Apple Preserves (page 63)

★ **Honey:** Herb-Infused Orange Honey (page 74)

★ **Gravy:** Sweet Potato Coconut Gravy (page 53)

★ **Butter:** Marcona Almond Butter (page 67) or Apricot White Ale Butter (page 66)

ROASTED CORN
AND JALAPEÑO BISCUIT

Yield: 6 large (5-ounce) biscuits

This biscuit is somewhere between cornbread and a biscuit. The char flavor from the grilled corn and jalapeños reminds us of grilling in the great outdoors and the time we spent out West. This biscuit is actually a mash-up of sorts between the South and the Southwest, and we use it for building a savory sandwich that leans either way. Oh, this biscuit also lends itself well to the addition of cheese! So if you are feeling adventurous, go ahead and throw in a handful of your favorite.

Ingredients

2 ears sweet corn

4 jalapeños

   Oil for grilling

   Salt and pepper

3 cups all-purpose flour (we use White Lily brand)

2 cups finely ground yellow cornmeal

1 tablespoon salt

1 tablespoon sugar

1 teaspoon whole cumin seed, toasted and ground

   Note: You can toast ground cumin as well if you watch it closely and toast it fast.

1 ½ tablespoons baking powder

8 tablespoons (1 stick) butter, chilled and cubed

2 tablespoons chopped cilantro

2 cups buttermilk

OPTIONAL:

1 ½ cups shredded pepper jack or smoked Cheddar

Prepare the Corn and Jalapeños

Heat up your grill to a nice high temperature. If you don't have a grill or you're cooking indoors, you can roast the corn and jalapeños under the broiler in your oven. Turn the broiler to high and get the vegetables nice and close—but not too close!—so they get a nice char.

While you're waiting for the grill or broiler to heat up, shuck the corn and clean off any strands. Toss the corn and the whole jalapeños in some oil and season with salt and pepper.

Once the grill or broiler is hot, cook the corn and the jalapeños. Char them a bit on all sides, keeping a close eye on them and rotating them with grill tongs whenever needed.

Once they are charred but not burnt, remove the vegetables from the grill and let them cool. If you want, you can start making the dry mix for the biscuits while you wait.

RECIPE CONTINUES

ROASTED CORN AND JALAPEÑO BISCUIT
(CONTINUED)

Once the corn is cool, cut the kernels off the cob and set aside. Now you have a decision to make—how hot do you want these biscuits? That's *your* call! If you want them hot, dice the peppers with all the seeds in. If you want less spice, split the peppers in half lengthwise, scrape the seeds out, and then dice them. Jalapeños can vary greatly in heat, so use your best judgment. Dice them up well and set aside with the corn.

Make the Biscuits

Preheat your oven to 375°F, making sure you have one of the racks in the middle of the oven. Grease a baking sheet or cast-iron skillet (pan spray works fine).

In a large mixing bowl, combine the flour, cornmeal, salt, sugar, cumin, and baking powder—mix completely.

Snap the butter into the dry ingredients (see page 26) and then mix in your pepper and corn mixture. Slowly fold in the cilantro and buttermilk, taking care not to overmix. Use a large ice cream scoop to get the dough into your pan or skillet. Make sure to keep the dough scoops right next to each other on the pan. (See the photo on page 27 for an example of how to space the biscuit dough.)

Bake 20 to 25 minutes or until golden brown.

Pairing Ideas

We love this biscuit smeared with any one of our pimento cheeses (page 86). We also like topping it with the Bacon-Wrapped Pork Loin with Smoked Maple Syrup (page 122) and a poached egg. The sweet, salty, spicy combo sets it over the top and is just perfection!

OTHER FAVORITES:

★ **Jam:** Honeycrisp Apple Preserves (page 63)
★ **Honey:** Chile Garlic Honey (page 76)
★ **Gravy:** Pork Sausage Gravy (page 52)—though we'd recommend the addition of green chiles to the gravy too!
★ **Butter:** Apricot White Ale Butter (page 66)

BEER CITY BISCUIT

Yield: 6 large (5-ounce) biscuits

Biscuit Head was born in Asheville, North Carolina, a city known as the home of the Blue Ridge Mountains, the Biltmore estate, and of course, *beer*. We have so many craft breweries in town, we were even voted Beer City, USA! Of course, we take pride in our mountain town and love the many libations and elixirs that are created here. So Asheville, this biscuit is for you.

Ingredients

- 1 cup cooked whole-grain barley (this can be cooked ahead of time and stored in the fridge)
- 4 cups all-purpose flour (we use White Lily brand)
- 1 cup whole wheat flour
- 1 tablespoon salt
- 1½ tablespoons baking powder
- 1 tablespoon nutritional yeast (optional)
- 1 tablespoon cocoa powder
- 8 tablespoons (1 stick) butter, chilled and cubed
- 1 cup whole buttermilk
- 1 cup chocolate porter

   Note: That's only 8 ounces, so go ahead and drink the remaining beer!

- 3 tablespoons blackstrap molasses

About the biscuit—it's a whole-grain base with an infusion of chocolate porter and molasses. We think you'll find it's a hearty and full-flavored biscuit that also goes perfectly with a pint. If you live close to a brewery and can sneak in on brew day, you can substitute the cooked barley with spent barley from the brewer. Just make sure you get it soon after the mash is finished so it's fresh.

Preheat your oven to 375°F, making sure you have one of the racks in the middle of the oven. Grease a baking sheet or cast-iron skillet (pan spray works fine).

Check your barley. It should be cooked well but not very wet.

Add both flours, salt, baking powder, nutritional yeast, and cocoa powder to a large bowl and sift.

Snap the butter into the dry ingredients (see page 26). Fold in the barley, buttermilk, and porter, then gently fold in the molasses. Be careful not to overmix!

Use a large ice cream scoop to place the dough into your pan or skillet. Make sure to keep the scoops of dough right next to each other on the pan. (See the photo on page 27 for an example of how to space the biscuit dough.)

Bake for 20 to 25 minutes or until dark golden brown.

Pairing Ideas

This biscuit lends itself well to a ploughman's style lunch with a big hunk of cheese or one of our pimento recipes (page 86) and pickles or Southern Chow Chow (page 139). This biscuit also goes well with almost anything sweet.

OTHER FAVORITES:

★ **Jam:** Raspberry Jam (page 61)

★ **Honey:** Roasted Honey with Thyme (page 75)

★ **Gravy:** Red Eye Gravy (page 51)

★ **Butter:** Raspberry Truffle Butter (page 71)

CHAPTER 2

On Your Biscuit

At Biscuit Head, we love to play with our food. And when it comes to playing with food, we probably have the most fun with all the stuff we put on top of our biscuits. We smother them with flavored butters. We drizzle them with infused honeys. We spread on jams ranging from simple classics to off-the-wall flavors. Oh, and don't forget about our never-ending rotation of hot sauce ranging from mild to melt-your-face, all with uniquely addicting flavors. We like to put those on our biscuits too.

If you've ever been to our restaurant, you probably could have guessed that we had an obsession with all these yummy toppings. Our jam bar is packed with many of our favorites as well as our flavors of the moment. It's like a crazy flavor lab for our chefs, and the only rule is that there are no rules!

In this chapter, we will teach you some basic techniques for making these goodies at home, along with that other signature biscuit topping: gravy! Flip through the pages and get inspired. We think that we have included something for everyone, whether you enjoy traditional and familiar flavors or are feeling a bit more adventurous.

GRAVIES

It doesn't get much better than rich, creamy gravy smothered over a nice crusty buttermilk biscuit. It's the perfect comfort food. In fact, we love it so much that at the restaurant we always have plenty to choose from, including the house favorites you'll find on the pages that follow. We also serve gravies of the day, which are rarely repeated but often a showcase for our chefs' creativity or a seasonal ingredient. After you make the gravies that follow, think about using one of them as a base recipe for your own creative gravy of the day!

For the true gravy lover, at the restaurant we even offer a flight of three different gravies to sample with your biscuits. Like a flight of beer at a craft brewery's taproom, the gravy flight is all about different tastes with every bite. The next time you're hosting brunch, consider trying something similar at home. Gravy is relatively easy to make, and you'll find that it's a sure-fire way to elevate a plate of humble biscuits to a spread that gets people talking!

RED EYE GRAVY

Yield: 5 cups (6 servings)

Red eye gravy has its roots in the Great Depression, when the recipe was created with resourcefulness in mind. The leftover coffee and cured ham were ingredients that could last a while without refrigeration. If you're not already familiar with this gravy, red eye should be thin, almost the consistency of au jus, because it's not thickened with flour like many other gravies. While the traditional base is country ham and coffee, we also add molasses, onion, and garlic to create a brighter, more balanced flavor. This is one of the easiest gravies to make, yet in our opinion it's still one of the best. We love the intense salty flavor once it soaks into a biscuit—and many swear by its ability to cure a hangover!

Ingredients

- 3 ounces country ham, chopped
- ¼ cup water
- ½ cup diced onion
- 1 teaspoon minced garlic
- 2 tablespoons molasses
- 4 cups brewed coffee
  (left over from the same day is fine)

Note: Country ham is an amazing ham that is becoming much more widely available throughout the United States. It is salt-cured and aged, making it more similar to a prosciutto than to the common ham served at Easter. It was created in the rural South as a means to save ham without refrigeration and have it last into the winter months. Country ham has a very distinct flavor that is not easily replicated with any other ingredient. Check with your local butcher or order online if you have to!

In a medium-sized cast-iron skillet, combine the country ham and water. Place over medium heat and let the mixture start to warm. Continue cooking until all the water has evaporated from the pan—in effect rendering the fat. Once the water has cooked out, let the ham crisp a little in its own fat.

Add the onion and garlic; sauté until it smells amazing but not long enough to brown. Add the molasses, stirring until it reaches a slight bubble. Add the coffee, bring back up to a simmer, and it's ready to serve!

PORK SAUSAGE GRAVY

Yield: 6 cups (6 servings)

Sometimes classics are classics for a reason! Our take on Southern pork sausage gravy has been the most popular gravy at our restaurant from day one. The creamy base you'll make here can be used to make many other types of gravy as well, including mushroom herb, veggie sausage, and even fried chicken gravy. Use your imagination and invent a new gravy!

Ingredients

- 1 pound breakfast sausage, hot or mild
- ½ cup all-purpose flour
- 4 cups whole milk
- ½ teaspoon kosher salt
- 2 teaspoons black pepper
- ½ teaspoon red pepper flakes
- Pinch of finely chopped fresh thyme (optional)

Note: For a vegetarian version of this gravy, just omit the sausage and start with the roux. However, you will need to melt ½ cup of butter to replace the sausage fat that would otherwise be in the pot. We also suggest adding a vegetarian meat product like seitan or tempeh. Sautéed mushrooms are great as well.

In a saucepan or large skillet over medium heat, cook the sausage all the way through. Continue to cook until the meat browns slightly. Remove the sausage with a spatula or slotted spoon and transfer it to a bowl or plate. Leave the grease in the pot.

Still over medium heat, whisk the flour into the sausage grease until a doughy paste has formed. This mixture of fat and flour is known as a roux.

Slowly whisk the milk into your roux. Pour only about a cup of milk at a time and whisk well before adding another cup. Lightly simmer for 3 to 5 minutes while stirring continuously. This will cook out the taste of the flour and incorporate all the flavors.

Return the sausage to the gravy and finish by adding your salt, pepper, red pepper flakes, and thyme. Bring this mixture up to a light simmer and then remove from heat.

Unfortunately, no one has yet invented straws that are wide enough for this gravy, so enjoy it poured over a fresh-from-the-oven biscuit.

SWEET POTATO COCONUT GRAVY

Yield: 6 cups (6 servings)

We are obsessed with this gravy at Biscuit Head. It's our most nontraditional gravy, as it draws from the rich flavors of the Caribbean instead of the South. It's amazing poured over a biscuit or used as a sauce for fried chicken, catfish, and seitan "sausage," to name just a few things. We also have a secret about this gravy; it is actually gluten-free and vegan, making it a great fit for special diets.

Ingredients

¼ cup diced onion

1 medium-sized sweet potato, diced

1 tablespoon coconut oil

1 clove garlic, chopped

1 teaspoon freshly cracked black pepper

1 tablespoon kosher salt

1 teaspoon curry powder (madras style)

⅓ teaspoon pie spice (page 16)

½ teaspoon red pepper flakes

⅓ cup brown sugar

2 (14-ounce) cans coconut milk

In a large saucepan, sauté the onions and sweet potato in the coconut oil over medium-high heat. Cook until the onions and sweet potato start to get a little color, then add the garlic and cook long enough for everything to caramelize a bit.

Stir in the seasonings, spices, and brown sugar until it all melts together into your vegetables.

Now pour in the coconut milk, reduce heat to a low simmer, and cook for 30 minutes or until the sweet potatoes are completely cooked through. Serve immediately.

THAT'S OUR JAM (BAR)

When walking into Biscuit Head, you will soon discover that we are condiment freaks. Of course we have the staples like ketchup and sriracha, but we also make all of our own hot sauces, jams, jellies, preserves, and flavored butters. We have a whole bar dedicated to these toppings, where our customers can mix and match flavors to their hearts' content. We have something for everyone, from strawberry and blueberry jams for the traditionalists to Amaretto Marmalade (page 60) and Sweet Potato Chai Butter (page 62) for the more adventurous. In this section, we're going to teach you about basic canning and share some of our favorite fruit preserve recipes as well.

First, we want to start by saying that you can make any of our jam or hot sauce recipes and simply refrigerate them for up to 2 weeks. The canning information is just for the folks who want to save them for longer. Second, a quick disclaimer: we are only going to be canning foods in this book that have a high acid content. The canning methods described are for these foods only and not to be used for foods that have low acidity. The acid in con-junction with the canning will help to preserve food and keep bacteria at bay. So, while in the rest of the book we encourage you to play with the recipes and substitute at will, we actually can't recommend doing that in this section unless you already have a good foundation of canning knowledge.

Let's start off with some basic classifications:

★ **Jelly** is made with the juice of fruit, sugar, and pectin.

★ **Jam** is made with the fruit itself, as well as its juice, sugar, and sometimes pectin.

★ **Preserves** are the same as jam but typically have larger pieces of fruit.

★ **Marmalade** is a combination of citrus fruit, citrus peel, and sugar.

★ **Fruit butter** is a spread made from fruit and sugar cooked into a paste (apple butter is the most well-known, but you can also use winter squash, sweet potatoes, carrots, and more).

If you've never canned, you probably recognized all those words except for one: pectin. Pectin is the gel part of the jelly. It comes naturally in some fruits, or you can add it in liquid or powdered form to create a gel in the fruit's liquid. Fruits that are naturally high in pectin—such as grapes, apple, citrus, and cherries—often do not need to have pectin added because they have enough in their skins to form a good gel.

HOW TO CAN

Now that we have that out of the way, let's get to canning! Canning is essentially a way to preserve and store food for use at a later time. Learning basic canning techniques will enable you to make things like jams, relishes, pickles, and much more and enjoy them throughout the year. If there is a local farm that has beautiful ripe blueberries or apples, you will be able to save them to enjoy in the dead of the winter—or to share them with friends and family, of course. Canning may seem time-consuming or difficult to do, but we're here to tell you that it's quite simple. Once you do it a few times, you'll probably even enjoy the process!

You Will Need

Large canning pot with lid

Canning rack

Jarring tongs

Mason jars with lids and rings

Note: The size and quantity of jars will depend on the size of your recipe and your personal preference. If it's being given as a gift or party favor, you may want to go with a smaller jar, but if you're saving it for yourself, a larger jar will make more sense. Just know that a wide-mouth jar will be much easier and cleaner to fill. Also, make sure that you always use new lids. You can reuse the jars and rings. However, you can't reuse the lids because the wax seal on them will only work one time.

Instructions

Step 1: Fill your canning pot halfway with tap water and place your empty jars, lids, and rings inside. They should be completely submerged in the water. Bring the water to a simmer.

Step 2: Before the water comes to a boil, remove the lids and canning rings and set them aside on a clean surface.

Step 3: Carefully remove the jars from the simmering water with jarring tongs and pour out any water in the jars. Ladle the jam or hot sauce right into the warm jars, leaving a ¼-inch headspace at the top of each jar. Immediately place the lids on the jars and screw the rings on tight.

Note: If you spill some jam down the side of the jar, wipe it with a damp, clean, hot towel.

Step 4: Return the filled and lidded jars to the pot and make sure they are submerged under 2 inches of water. Bring the water to a boil, uncovered. Then cover with the pot's lid and boil for 10 minutes.

Step 5: After 10 minutes, carefully remove the jars and place on a towel to cool. You are finished! The jam or hot sauce should store for up to a year and allow you to enjoy your goodies later on.

SPICED CHERRY JAM

Yield: 4 pints

The spiced cherry jam is always popular and disappears quickly from our jam bar at the restaurant when cherries are in season. The spices complement rather than hide the cherry flavor and elevate the recipe from your typical plain jam—it's perfect for the fall season. Try it on a biscuit with some butter or baste it on meats like duck or roasted pork as a finishing glaze.

Ingredients

- 2 pounds fresh cherries, washed and pitted (sour or sweet—you can use frozen if fresh aren't available)
- 1 tablespoon Pie Spice (page 16)
- 2 tablespoons sorghum or molasses
- Zest of 1 lemon
- 4 cups sugar

Add your cherries to a large saucepan with the pie spice, molasses, and zest. When selecting your pot, keep in mind that the jam will double in size when it bubbles up during cooking.

Over medium-high heat, bring the mixture to a light boil.

Stir in the sugar and continue to cook for 20 to 30 minutes. Starting at 20 minutes, or when the jam darkens in color and coats the back of a spoon, use the freezer-plate method below to check if it's done.

You can serve this jam hot or cold, so serve immediately or transfer to jars and refrigerate for up to 2 weeks. If you'd like to can your batch of jam instead, see page 56.

The Freezer-Plate Method

There are many factors that can make a jam recipe cook at different speeds for different people. The size of the pot, the temperature, and the water content of the fruit can all affect cooking times. So how do you tell if your jam is done?

Here is a foolproof way to know: the freezer-plate method. Place a plate in the freezer for about 15 minutes. This works out, more or less, to a few minutes after the time you start boiling your jam. Once your jam has cooked for 20 to 30 minutes, take the plate out and put a spoonful of hot jam onto it. Allow it to sit for about 20 seconds, then run one finger down the middle of the jam. If the finger swipe mark stays, the jam is done! If the jam runs back into the mark, it needs to cook longer. It really is that easy.

AMARETTO MARMALADE

Yield: 6 pints

This marmalade has become one of our most popular jams and a staple on our jam bar. It's fun and unique but still has that marmalade flavor that citrus lovers enjoy. We serve fresh-squeezed orange juice at the restaurant, so this was also a natural way to use all the leftover pulp and rinds. Pour this over some of our Buttermilk Ice Cream (page 195) for a special treat!

Ingredients

- 5 to 6 medium oranges (use more or less depending on size)
- 8 cups sugar
- 2 tablespoons amaretto
- 1 teaspoon almond extract

Wash the oranges with warm water. Cut them into quarters and remove any visible seeds. Sometimes you'll get some really seedy ones, so if that's the case, juice them first, remove the seeds, and proceed with the recipe.

Pulse the orange quarters (yes, including the peels) in a food processor until they are chopped into small pieces.

Combine the orange mixture with the sugar and amaretto in a large saucepan and simmer over medium heat. The mixture will double or triple in size, so choose your pan accordingly. It should cook for about 20 to 30 minutes. Starting at 20 minutes, or when the bubbles get smaller and the mixture begins to darken, use the freezer-plate method (page 59) to check if it's done. Once it's ready, stir in the almond extract and remove from the heat.

While the marmalade is still warm, transfer it to jars and then place them in the fridge. It will keep for up to 2 weeks. If you'd like to can your batch of marmalade instead, see page 56.

RASPBERRY JAM

Yield: 8 pints

While we love coming up with fun and unique flavors, sometimes you just can't beat the classics—and our raspberry jam is one of the best. This is an all-time crowd pleaser with a beautiful color, flavor, and aroma. Can it and enjoy the bright, summery raspberry flavor even in the middle of winter.

Ingredients

- 4 cups fresh raspberries (you can substitute frozen if they're out of season)
- 1 tablespoon freshly squeezed lemon juice
- 1 packet (1.75 ounces) pectin
- 6 cups sugar

Combine the raspberries and lemon juice in a medium to large saucepan, keeping in mind that this recipe will double in size as it cooks. Mash the raspberries up a bit with the back of a large wooden spoon.

Cook the mixture, stirring constantly, over medium-high heat until it comes to a light boil.

Once it's boiling, add the pectin and continue to stir while slowly adding the sugar. Once the sugar has dissolved, turn off the heat.

While the jam is still warm, transfer it to jars and place them in the fridge. It will keep for about 2 weeks. If you'd like to can your batch of jam instead, see page 56.

SWEET POTATO CHAI BUTTER

Yield: 5 pints

This flavorful fruit butter is made in the same way as an apple butter, but we use sweet potatoes for their amazing flavor and creamy, smooth texture. We add chai spices to it for a unique flavor that's reminiscent of the fall, but tastes good any time of the year. It's an example of how way more than just apples and pears can be cooked with sugar and whipped into a tasty spread.

Ingredients

5 cups peeled and large-diced sweet potato

4 cups light brown sugar

½ tablespoon ground cinnamon

1 teaspoon vanilla extract

½ teaspoon ground allspice

½ teaspoon ground nutmeg

½ teaspoon salt

¼ teaspoon ground cloves

Place the sweet potatoes in a medium-sized pot and cover with cold water. Set the pot on the stove with the heat set to medium high. Cover the pot with a tight-fitting lid and cook the sweet potatoes until they can be easily pierced with a fork.

Once the sweet potatoes are cooked, turn off the stove, remove the pot, and drain the potatoes.

Return the potatoes to the pot or place in a large mixing bowl. Add the rest of the ingredients and mix them together very well. We recommend using an immersion blender to really purée them, but you could also use a hand mixer or just transfer the mixture to a standard blender and purée. The idea is that you want a smooth sweet potato paste with all the brown sugar melted into the hot sweet potato.

At this point, you can chill your mixture and then enjoy! Just like the other jams, this will keep in the fridge for 2 weeks. This recipe does not can well due to the low acid content. Still, it's so delicious that chances are it won't be around that long anyway!

HONEYCRISP APPLE PRESERVES

Yield: 5 pints

North Carolina's farmers grow a wide variety of delicious apples. One of our personal favorites is the Honeycrisp. Every fall we travel to local farms and pick bags of them to bring home. It's an apple that is delicious on its own, but it also holds up well to the long cooking time of this preserve recipe.

Ingredients

4 large Honeycrisp apples
(about 5 cups once prepared)

1 cup water

5 cups sugar

Juice of 1 lemon

1 teaspoon Pie Spice (page 16)

To prepare the apples, peel and cut them off the core, cutting around the core so that each apple ends up in four nice pieces. Dice these into 1-inch cubes. You should have 5 cups.

In a medium saucepan, heat the water, sugar, and lemon juice over medium-high heat, stirring until dissolved. Once the sugar is dissolved, slowly add the apple pieces. Bring the mixture to a boil, giving it a stir every once in a while.

Once a boil is reached, reduce the mixture to a simmer over low heat and cook for about 45 minutes. The preserve should thicken nicely, but test it with the freezer-plate method (page 59). Once the preserve passes the test, stir in the Pie Spice and remove it from the heat.

While warm, transfer the mixture to jars and then place them in the fridge. The jam will keep for about 2 weeks. If you'd like to can your batch of jam instead, see page 56.

WHIP IT REAL GOOD
(THE BUTTER, THAT IS)

Sure, you might think the star of a jam bar would be, well, jam. However, for some of our regulars the trip to the jam bar starts and ends with our flavored compound butters. Compound butters might sound complicated, but it's actually relatively simple to make most of them. All you really need on hand is softened butter and your imagination. At the restaurant we mix these up by hand, but a food processor, stand mixer, or hand mixer will all work as well.

We often do small batches, and the flavors are always changing. On any given day, you might find butters with candy bars, Pop Rocks, durian fruit, maple bacon, or blue cheese and wing sauce. The recipes that follow are some of our all-time favorites, though, and they show up on the bar regularly.

APRICOT WHITE ALE BUTTER

Yield: 2 cups

This sweet spread is almost a jam-butter hybrid thanks to the large proportion of apricots. It has a perfect balance of earthy beer, vanilla sweetness, honey, fruit, and just a touch of cardamom spice. This is a delicious butter spread for your biscuit brunch, but it also pairs well with fish.

Ingredients

12 ounces white ale or hefeweizen

½ pound dried, sulfate-free apricots

¼ cup honey

1 teaspoon vanilla extract

2 sticks salted butter

Pinch of ground cardamom

Salt and pepper, to taste

In a medium-sized saucepan, add the beer, apricots, honey, and vanilla; cook over medium heat, bringing the mixture to a simmer. Cook until the beer is almost completely reduced and the apricots have a glazed sheen.

Cool the mixture down by setting the pan directly inside a large bowl of ice and stir the mixture to quickly release the heat. The mixture needs to be at room temperature or cooler so you don't melt the butter in the next step.

Puree the apricot ale reduction in a food processor or blender. Add the butter, cardamom, salt, and pepper to the processor and pulse gently to incorporate.

Store in the refrigerator in an airtight container for up to 2 weeks.

MARCONA ALMOND BUTTER

Yield: 2 ½ cups

This recipe will make you forget all about regular old peanut butter. Make a batch of this, and you'll find yourself eating it by the spoonful. It also pairs great on a plate with a biscuit, the Bourbon Figs (see page 196), and a nice French cheese like reblochon or bocheron.

Ingredients

2 cups marcona almonds

¼ cup canola oil

¼ cup molasses

1 teaspoon salt

Toast the almonds in a 350° F oven until they are a nice toasty brown but not burnt.

Add the toasted almonds to your food processor and blend with the oil, molasses, and salt until creamy. This can be stored at room temperature, covered, and will last several months. It does tend to separate over time, so you may have to mix it back up.

SRIRACHA HONEY BUTTER

Yield: 3/4 cup

Sriracha is one of our go-to condiments because of its unmatched spicy, fermented flavor. For those who don't like a lot of heat but still want a little bit of that funky punch, this butter will be perfect. Sweetening it with the honey rounds out the flavor and makes it a perfect spread.

Ingredients

- 8 tablespoons (1 stick) salted butter, softened
- 1 tablespoon sriracha
- 2 tablespoons honey (we prefer clover honey for this recipe)
- 1 tablespoon sesame seeds, toasted

If your butter is soft enough, all you need to do for this recipe is stir all the ingredients into the butter with a spatula. If the butter isn't quite soft enough or you're struggling to get everything combined by hand, a stand mixer with a paddle attachment, a blender, or hand mixer will do the trick.

Once the ingredients are fully incorporated, it's ready to spread! This can be stored in the fridge for several weeks but is best served at room temperature. Be sure to pull it out to warm back up before you use it!

RASPBERRY TRUFFLE BUTTER

Yield: 1½ cups

Raspberries. Chocolate. Butter. With three of the greatest things in the world, this recipe will not disappoint. This butter may cause you to scour your kitchen, looking for any possible food to dip into it. A dollop of this butter on a hot biscuit with some fresh raspberries? Pure magic.

Ingredients

½ pint raspberries (about 3 ounces)

½ cup sugar

1 tablespoon raspberry liquor (we use Chambord)

2 tablespoons cocoa powder

8 tablespoons (1 stick) salted butter, softened

In a small saucepan, heat the raspberries and sugar over low heat until the raspberries begin to release some of their juice. At that point, stir the mixture and turn the heat up a bit to medium, stirring gently until the sugar is dissolved.

Once the sugar has melted, add the raspberry liquor and cocoa powder and take the pan off the heat. Stir to incorporate all the ingredients and to cool the mixture down a bit faster. Once it's cool, stir the mixture into the butter with a spatula. Store covered in the fridge for several weeks, though this is best served at room temperature.

INFUSED HONEYS

What goes better with biscuits and butter than honey? Not much! Honey can come in a wide range of flavors depending on what type of flower the bees were getting their pollen from. For example, if you buy clover honey, bees made the honey while pollinating the clover flower, whereas chestnut honey is made by bees that live near and pollinate the flowers of the chestnut tree. So honey, like wine, is affected by its terroir, or the environment from which it comes. The honey will differ in shades, aromas, thickness, and flavor. Some honeys will be a touch sweeter, or have a hint of tart blueberry or orange, while some will have a more robust floral taste. So go out and try some different honeys and enjoy all of the sweetness of the bees' hard work.

For our blended honeys, we recommend using plain old clover honey, as it has a subtler flavor. If you're adding another flavor to something, it's best to start with more of a blank canvas. Another perk of clover honey is that it tends to be less expensive. Because you're adding flavors, there's no need to pay a premium for a honey varietal with subtle flavors you're going to cover up.

HERB-INFUSED ORANGE HONEY

Yield: 1 cup

Whether you want the earthy, piney touch of rosemary or the floral, sweet scent of lavender, this recipe will deliver the goods. It's kind of a choose-your-own-honey adventure, so try whichever herb you like best! A hot, fresh biscuit broken open with a little butter and a big scoop of this honey makes for a great start to your day.

Ingredients

1 cup honey, your choice

1 ½ tablespoons freshly gathered lavender flowers
   or 1 ½ teaspoons rosemary leaves
   (or experiment with the fresh herb of your choice)

   Zest and juice of 1 orange

1 teaspoon cracked black pepper

In a microwavable bowl, heat the honey for 30 seconds. Stir in the other ingredients and pour into a Mason jar.

This honey is best served warm but is still delicious at room temperature. With a tight-fitting lid, it will keep for up to a month in your pantry.

ROASTED HONEY WITH THYME

Yield: 1 cup

This honey brings to mind a thick caramel, which makes for a wonderful spread. The roasting of the honey gives it a nutty richness as well and makes it an excellent match for biscuits, come autumn. We think it's perfect drizzled over fried chicken any time of the year!

Ingredients

1 cup honey

½ tablespoon thyme leaves

2 tablespoons heavy cream

Pinch of kosher salt

To roast and slightly burn the honey, heat it up in a medium saucepan until it starts to froth and come to a slight boil. Reduce the heat to a simmer and stir, watching it until it starts to turn brown and smoke ever so slightly. Immediately take it off the heat and stir in the thyme leaves and cream.

Scrape the mixture into a Mason jar to serve and store. It's best served warm and is easy to reheat by popping in the microwave for 15 to 20 seconds. In a jar with a tight-fitting lid, this honey will keep at room temperature for about a month.

CHILE GARLIC HONEY

Yield: 1¼ cup

Spicy and sweet, this honey really does hurt so good. Of all the honeys, it packs the biggest punch and is for those who enjoy the boldest flavors. We like to pour this honey over fried chicken or our Chicken-Fried Tofu (see page 98). It also complements the Okra Hush Puppies (see page 143).

Ingredients

- 1 cup honey
- ¼ cup sambal oelek (a chile garlic paste that can be found in the Asian section of most stores)
- Juice of ½ lime
- 1 clove garlic, minced

Combine all ingredients in a small saucepan and cook over low heat for 5 minutes. Pour into a Mason jar to serve or store. With a tight-fitting lid, this honey keeps at room temperature for up to a month.

HOT SAUCES

Hot sauce is such a fun condiment. It adds not only flavor to a dish, but also a feeling. Hot sauce can literally change your attitude! It's true; spicy foods can increase your endorphin levels and change your mood. That is pretty powerful stuff. At times, we'll have more than a dozen different homemade hot sauces floating around the restaurant for people to sample. However, the few that follow are our house recipes, our staples. They're the all-time favorites that we're afraid to discontinue lest we cause a hot sauce riot.

Thanks to their low pH and high acid content, many hot sauces do not need to be refrigerated. However, please keep in mind that the pH can vary greatly depending on the sauce and the ingredients in it, and some do need to be refrigerated and will have different shelf lives. As with the jams, we do not encourage you to experiment with these recipes if you intend to keep them around for more than a few days. The storage and shelf life information for each individual recipe is accurate but unfortunately will not apply if you tweak the recipes.

BLUEBERRY JALAPEÑO HOT SAUCE

Yield: 1 quart

Ingredients

½ pound jalapeño peppers

1 cup blueberries

½ cup apple cider vinegar

1 cup water

¼ onion, diced

2 tablespoons salt

1 ½ tablespoons brown sugar

1 clove garlic

½ teaspoon ground cumin

½ teaspoon ground coriander

¼ teaspoon ground allspice

¼ teaspoon xanthan gum

Note: The xanthan gum can be omitted. It's an emulsifier that helps keep the sauce from separating in the bottle. You can find it at most health food stores under the Bob's Red Mill brand. If you don't use it, you will just need to shake the hot sauce before using it.

Clean the peppers and remove the stems. Give them a rough chop and transfer them to a medium-sized saucepan with all the remaining ingredients except the xanthan gum. Turn the heat on the burner to medium-low. Bring the sauce to a gentle, low simmer and then cook, with the lid on, for about an hour.

After an hour, remove the pot from the heat. Add the xanthan gum, if using, and give it a spin with an immersion blender until smooth. (You can also transfer it to a conventional blender, but be careful not to stain your clothes with a splashy transfer!)

Transfer with a funnel into clean hot sauce bottles or Mason jars. This sauce can be kept at room temperature, but we recommend storing it in the fridge, where it will keep for up to 2 months.

STRAWBERRY BUFFALO SAUCE

Yield: 1 quart

This is our fruity variation of a classic buffalo sauce: buttery, tart, and spicy. People go crazy for this sauce because it's based on such a familiar, iconic flavor. Yet it's just different enough, due to the addition of the fruit and seasonings, to make it a little unexpected as well. Like most store-bought buffalo sauce, it has a mild to medium heat level that most people can handle without breaking too much of a sweat. It's a go-to sauce with anything fried as well as most any meat.

Ingredients

2 cups Frank's RedHot sauce

¼ cup water

15 strawberries, tops removed

8 tablespoons (1 stick) butter

5 cloves garlic, thinly sliced

1 teaspoon ground coriander

⅛ teaspoon ground cinnamon

1 teaspoon ground cumin

¼ teaspoon salt

½ teaspoon cracked black pepper

In a high-sided mixing bowl or saucepan, combine the Frank's RedHot sauce, water, and strawberries. Set aside.

In a medium-sized sauté pan over medium heat, melt the butter. Slowly stir the butter until the milk solids start to get a little toasty and you can smell the aroma of nuts. Once you just begin to notice the butter changing color, add the garlic and all of the spices and cook for 1 minute, or just enough to toast the spices and garlic in the quickly browning butter. Remove from the heat.

Here comes the tricky part. If it's the first time you're making this recipe, four hands are better than two, so you might want to enlist a friend. Slowly drizzle the butter into the hot sauce while blending with an immersion blender. The trick to getting the sauce to stay together (or emulsifying it) is to pour the butter very slowly, just a drizzle. Do not stop blending until all of the butter is added.

Pour the finished product into Mason jars, hot sauce bottles, or squeeze bottles. This sauce can be stored at room temperature, but we recommend storing it in the fridge, where it will keep for up to 2 months.

D'ARBOL SAUCE

Yield: 3 cups

This pepper sauce has some really complex flavors as well as a good amount of heat, thanks to the chile de arbol (pronounced "day are ball"). You can find these dried chiles in most grocery stores in large bags. If you are having trouble finding them, your local Hispanic market will have them or you can order them online.

Ingredients

- 1 cup firmly packed chiles de arbol, stems removed
- 1 teaspoon coriander seeds
- 1 cup apple cider vinegar
- ½ cup water
- 2 cloves garlic, finely chopped
- Zest and juice of 1 orange
- 1 tablespoon chopped fresh cilantro
- 2 tablespoons salt

In a medium-sized saucepan, toast the dry chiles over high heat until the seeds start to pop. Once toasted, transfer the peppers to a food processor or blender.

Add the coriander seeds to the pan and toast over high heat until fragrant. Turn off the heat and add the coriander to the food processor or blender. Add the remaining ingredients and purée until smooth.

Strain through a fine-mesh sieve into a large measuring cup with a spout. You want to get all the seeds and skins out and retain only the sauce. The best way to strain it is to pour into the strainer and use a rubber spatula to scrape it back and forth, pushing the sauce through. Press the mixture until all the liquid comes out.

Transfer the sauce to clean hot sauce bottles or Mason jars. Like the other hot sauces, this can be kept at room temperature, but we recommend storing it in the fridge, where it will keep for up to 2 months.

CHAPTER 3

In Your Biscuit

Now that you have the basics of biscuit making down and you've had some fun whipping up all sorts of gravies and toppings, you're ready for more. In this chapter we'll teach you some of our all-time favorites, like Mimosa Fried Chicken and Hoop and Jalapeño Pimento Cheese. We'll also share some of our most popular specials, like Bacon-Wrapped Pork Loin and Duck Confit Hash.

What do all these recipes have in common? You spread or stack them on a biscuit, of course! It's no secret that we love to use biscuits in place of bread. We might be biased, but we think they make for a buttery, flaky, and delicious base for all sorts of sandwiches. Look no further than the classic breakfast sandwich; eggs, Cheddar, and bacon practically scream for a biscuit. But of course we go far beyond the classics. We serve all sorts of Benedicts, and on any given day you might find deep-fried tofu, fried green tomatoes, or fried catfish and sofrito atop a biscuit. On page 30, we have a cheat sheet for one of our sandwiches, but we encourage you to use the meaty mains and other recipes in this chapter in your own creations. Find what calls to you and then flip through the book to find another recipe or two that pairs with it. Be a sandwich inventor!

PIMENTO CHEESE

Pimento Cheese is sometimes lovingly referred to as the "caviar of the South." Although we think giving local trout roe that title makes more sense, we can understand the pride and adoration behind the saying. Jason grew up eating pimento cheese sandwiches that his mother prepared in a classic and simple way, and we still look forward to eating them at her house to this day; the recipe is just white bread, mayo, shredded Cheddar, and pimentos (OK, and maybe a little Texas Pete if you're feeling adventurous).

There's something about biting into a sandwich just the way your mom made it that takes you right back to being a kid. This is why so many Southerners have such a nostalgic reverence for this classic spread and why we knew it absolutely needed to be on our menu at Biscuit Head.

Pimento cheese can be used in a million different ways, and we love to add it to lots of different dishes at the restaurant and at home. We use it on our pulled pork biscuit to add creamy, cheesy amazingness. A dollop on top of grits or in scrambled eggs? Yes, please. Put out a bowl of it as a dip for crackers, pretzels, or fresh veggies at your next party and see how fast it disappears. It will soon become a staple no matter what part of the country you live in.

We are going to give you a few different recipes and variations of pimento cheese, but please, please, please feel free to be creative and add your own spin. If you love spice, add some extra hot peppers or hot sauce. If you love crunchy, smoky bacon, crumble some in! You'll find that there is something so rewarding about putting your own spin on this dish and watching people enjoy it. These recipes are guidelines, and you should use them to make your own "house" pimento cheese!

HOOP AND JALAPEÑO PIMENTO CHEESE

Yield: 4 cups (6 to 8 servings)

This recipe packs a little punch thanks to the jalapeños, but the peppers are more about adding to the complexity of the dip—it won't blow anyone away with spice. You'll find it has an amazing balance of textures and flavors that keeps you coming back for more.

Hoop cheese is a red-waxed cheese that you can find at farmers' markets and roadside stands throughout the South, and it's known for its creaminess and simplicity. It's made with cow's milk and is most similar to a farmer's cheese. Feel free to substitute a mild Cheddar or another favorite cheese along those lines if you can't find hoop cheese.

Ingredients

1 pound hoop cheese or mild Cheddar cheese, grated large

8 ounces cream cheese, at room temperature

½ cup mayonnaise (we use Duke's)

4 deseeded jalapeños, minced

   Note: If you want to make the recipe hotter, leave the seeds in.

1 clove garlic, minced

   Pinch of ground cumin

   Salt and pepper, to taste

In a large mixing bowl, combine all ingredients and stir together with a rubber spatula. Cover and refrigerate. This is traditionally served cold but is also served warm in grilled cheese sandwiches or stirred into grits. Pimento cheese will last for 1 week in an airtight container in the fridge.

CLASSIC PIMENTO CHEESE

Yield: 4 cups (6 to 8 servings)

This is the most traditional pimento cheese that we make. In fact, it's quite similar to the pimento cheese we both remember from our childhoods. The texture is creamy and soft, but the pecans bring a welcome crunch. If you want to dial up the spice, add some extra hot sauce!

Ingredients

4 ounces cream cheese, at room temperature

½ cup mayonnaise (we use Duke's)

1 tablespoon hot sauce

1 tablespoon molasses

¼ teaspoon smoked paprika

2 4-ounce jars diced pimentos, drained well

Note: If you can't find diced pimentos at the store, whole pimentos or roasted red peppers, diced, will be a great substitution.

1 pound sharp Cheddar cheese, grated large

Salt and freshly ground pepper to taste

In a large mixing bowl, combine the softened cream cheese, mayonnaise, hot sauce, molasses, and smoked paprika. Incorporate well.

Add the drained pimentos and the sharp Cheddar, a pinch of salt, and a couple turns of freshly cracked black pepper; mix well enough to incorporate the cheese and the pimentos with the cream cheese–mayonnaise mixture.

Cover and store, refrigerated, for up to 1 week. As with the other pimento cheeses, this is typically served cold but can also be enjoyed warmed in grilled cheese sandwiches or grits.

SMOKEHOUSE PIMENTO CHEESE

Yield: 4 cups (6 to 8 servings)

This is a smoky barbecue variation on pimento cheese. It has a sweet and smoky flavor with just enough kick from the chipotles. Try it as an addition to a hamburger, stir it into scrambled eggs, or let it be the star of the show and dip into it with warm flour tortillas.

Ingredients

4 ounces cream cheese, at room temperature

⅓ cup mayonnaise (we use Duke's)

1 tablespoon barbecue sauce

1 pound smoked Cheddar cheese, grated large

¼ cup cooked, crumbled bacon

2 chipotle peppers in adobo sauce, chopped

   Note: These peppers come out of a can coated in sauce. Don't wipe them off before chopping. Add the sauce coating to this recipe as well!

2 tablespoons finely chopped BBQ Pickled Onions (page 140)

Mix the cream cheese, mayonnaise, and barbecue sauce in a large mixing bowl, incorporating well.

Add the shredded cheese, bacon, chipotle peppers, and onions. Cover and refrigerate for up to 1 week.

MIMOSA FRIED CHICKEN

Yield: 4 servings

This is it: the secret recipe for our fried chicken. While many think of chicken breasts when it comes to fried chicken, we say you can't beat the chicken thigh. It is a more tender, moist, and flavorful cut—though if you really want to, you can substitute breast meat in this recipe. We source our meat locally and suggest you do the same. Antibiotic- and hormone-free chickens that have been raised the right way make a difference! As for the brine, don't skip it. That's the secret to infusing extra flavor and juiciness into the meat.

Ingredients

FOR THE BRINE:

2 tablespoons kosher salt

3 tablespoons sugar

2 teaspoons ground coriander

1 bay leaf

2 cups water

2 teaspoons paprika

1 teaspoon curry powder

2 cups orange juice

¼ cup champagne

FOR THE CHICKEN:

4 large boneless skinless chicken thighs

1 quart vegetable oil (or however much it takes to fill your fryer)

2 cups Biscuit Head Dredge (see sidebar on page 94)

Mix together all of the ingredients for the brine. Stir until the salt and sugar are dissolved, then place the chicken into the brine and set covered in the fridge overnight.

The next morning, it's time to pull out that chicken and fry it up! As a wise man once said, "Chicken ain't chicken 'til it's fried."

In your home fryer or a pot large enough to safely deep-fry, preheat your oil to 335°F.

Note: This recipe (and just about any deep fryer recipe) can also be cooked in a cast-iron skillet on the stove top. We recommend using lard if you go this route. Use enough so that the lard comes up at least halfway on what you're cooking—the goal is to flip just once.

RECIPE CONTINUES

MIMOSA FRIED CHICKEN (CONTINUED)

While your oil is heating up, remove the chicken from the brine and shake off any excess liquid. Completely coat the chicken in the dredge by shaking the thighs in a doubled-up disposable plastic grocery bag. This is the best way to do it at home, because your hands stay clean, and you can just throw the bag away when you're done.

Let the chicken thighs rest for 3 minutes in the dredge bag, then give them one more good shake in the dredge to make sure that they're fully coated. Now they're ready to fry. Carefully place each piece of chicken into the hot oil and fry away. Cooking for about 10 minutes should get the chicken right where you want it. You are looking for a nice golden crust and an internal temperature of 162°F. Remove the chicken from the oil and place on a wire rack to rest a few minutes—serve it while it's hot!

Southern-Fried Everything

Collards, kale, black-eyed peas, and butterbeans are all wonderful and have their place, but nothing beats a crispy piece of fried catfish or chicken. In these pages, we're sharing some of our favorite fried recipes with you, but once you get comfortable with the basic technique, you can certainly get creative with it.

To fry any food, it's all about two things: hot fat and some kind of dry coating or flour. There are countless oils or fats you could use, but our favorites are peanut oil, duck fat, and vegetable oil. Each oil or fat adds its own unique flavor, so it's up to you to choose whichever you like best.

Frying tip: While your oil is heating up, grab a sheet pan and put a wire resting rack on it. This is your go-to landing zone for most things fried.

For breading, you also have unlimited options. You can use anything from crushed cereal, to cookies or crackers, to ground rice or barley. We like to mix it up and use a variety of things, but our staple is our specially seasoned flour mixture or dredge.

Biscuit Head Dredge

Use this to coat anything savory that you want to fry.

8 cups all-purpose flour

¼ cup salt

1 tablespoon garlic powder

1 tablespoon ground smoked paprika

½ tablespoon ground cayenne pepper

2 teaspoons freshly ground black pepper

Sift everything together and mix well. Store in an airtight container for up to 1 year.

Chèvre Dressing

This is Biscuit Head's version of ranch dressing, but with an extra tangy kick from goat cheese. We always use Looking Glass Creamery's chèvre at the restaurant because it is such a high-quality and delicious cheese. If you can't find this where you live, we urge you to support your local farm and cheesemonger and get a locally made, artisan chèvre from your area! This recipe makes a lot of dressing but is great to have on hand to use as a dip or on salads.

2 cups mayonnaise (we use Duke's)

½ cup Greek yogurt

2 cups buttermilk

2 teaspoons garlic powder

½ teaspoon freshly ground black pepper

½ teaspoon smoked paprika

2 tablespoons apple cider vinegar

2 ½ teaspoons kosher salt

1 tablespoon chopped parsley

½ cup chèvre or smoked chèvre (page 129)

Zest and juice of 1 lemon

Combine all ingredients in a blender and blend until incorporated.

SOUTHERN FRIED GREEN TOMATOES
WITH CHÈVRE DRESSING

Yield: 4 to 6 servings

Underripe fruits like green tomatoes, green strawberries, and green mangoes are delicious and unique thanks to the tart and crisp qualities that set them apart from their ripe siblings. The flavor of a green tomato is like a lemony crisp pickle, but when it is fried, the tomato starts to break down and release some of its sugars; it then becomes a little sweeter. There is a moment in *The Simpsons* where Abu is asked about his favorite movie, book, and food, and he responds "Fried Green Tomatoes" to all three. After making this recipe, maybe you'll better understand one of his answers!

Ingredients

- 1 quart vegetable oil
  (or however much it takes to fill your fryer)
- 4 cups Biscuit Head Dredge (page 94)
- 4 large green tomatoes
- 4 eggs
- 1 ½ cups buttermilk
- 1 teaspoon Head Spice (page 16)

Start heating the oil in your deep fryer (or a pot or cast-iron skillet large enough to safely deep-fry) to 335°F.

Put the dredge in a big bowl. Slice the green tomatoes into ¼-inch slices and toss in the dredge until fully coated.

Crack and beat the eggs. Add the buttermilk and the Head Spice.

Remove the green tomatoes from the flour and coat in the egg-buttermilk mix. One at a time, transfer the battered green tomatoes back into the flour and press firmly until you have a solid coating.

Fry for 4 to 5 minutes or until golden brown.

CHICKEN-FRIED TOFU

Yield: 4 to 6 servings

This is a vegetarian dish that is sure to satisfy. By using corn flakes in the crust, you'll find that the tofu really pops with a crunchy and slightly sweet exterior. Top it with some veggie gravy (such as the Sweet Potato Coconut Gravy on page 53), and even meat eaters will be loving life! While tofu comes in a few different levels of firmness, we recommend sticking with extra-firm for this recipe.

Ingredients

- 2 blocks extra-firm tofu
- 2 cups buttermilk
- 3 tablespoons Head Spice (page 16)
- 2 cups flour

    Note: If you want an even sweeter crust, you can use pancake flour mix instead.

- 5 cups corn flakes
- 1 cup vegetable oil
  (or enough to fill your pan ½ inch)

Remove the tofu from its package and dump any tofu water down the drain. Cut the block in half width-wise and then cut each piece into 6 slices.

In a medium-sized mixing bowl, combine the buttermilk and Head Spice; add the tofu. Soak for 30 minutes. While the tofu is soaking, you can crush up all of the corn flakes and set them aside.

Heat the oil (making sure you have at least ½ inch) in a cast-iron skillet to 350°F. You can also deep-fry these little guys if you so choose, but we prefer the skillet for this recipe.

Prepare two separate medium-sized bowls, filling one with the flour and the other with the corn flakes. Remove the tofu from the buttermilk and toss it in the flour. Let it sit in the flour for a few minutes. Then toss the tofu back into the buttermilk, making sure to coat it well. Gently roll the tofu into the cornflakes and carefully place each piece into the hot oil.

Let the tofu brown, then gently turn the pieces over to brown on the other side. Once you have a nice golden crust (about 3 minutes per side), remove the tofu from your pan and let rest on a wire rack to cool slightly.

Smother the tofu in gravy and garnish with a couple of pickles.

BOILED PEANUT FALAFEL
WITH PEANUT BUTTER MOLASSES

Yield: 4 servings

Boiled peanuts are a Southern roadside phenomenon, and if you haven't had the pleasure of eating a bag, then be sure to make some extra to eat on their own when you try this recipe. They usually come in two different styles: regular and Cajun (spicy). Boiled peanuts are a lot different than the roasted ballpark variety. They are soft and have a texture similar to a cooked bean. You can buy your own ready to go or you can make them for this recipe. They do take a while to cook, so be prepared for the long haul when you are making these guys.

Ingredients

FOR THE BOILED PEANUTS:

2 pounds raw peanuts in the shell (sometimes labeled green peanuts)

½ cup kosher salt

2 tablespoons Head Spice (page 16)

2 cloves garlic, smashed

1 jalapeño pepper, split in half

1 bay leaf

Make the Boiled Peanuts

In a large pot, cover the peanuts with water and soak overnight. Make sure to weigh the nuts down with a plate or something heavy enough to keep them submerged. In the morning, drain the water and fill the pot back up with fresh water to cover the peanuts. Add the rest of the ingredients.

Bring this mixture to a boil, then cover and reduce to a simmer; let cook for about 5 hours. The peanuts are done when they have the firmness of a cooked bean. Make sure to check your water level every once in a while to make sure it doesn't reduce too far; you want your peanuts to stay submerged. Add more water if you need to.

This peanut elixir (the cooking water) is used for the molasses, and it's the perfect liquid to store your boiled peanuts in, so you'll want to save it. Cool and store in the liquid for up to 3 days.

RECIPE CONTINUES

BOILED PEANUT FALAFEL
WITH PEANUT BUTTER MOLASSES (CONTINUED)

FOR THE PEANUT BUTTER MOLASSES:

½ cup unsweetened peanut butter

¼ cup molasses

¼ cup peanut boil liquid

FOR THE FALAFEL:

1 quart vegetable oil (or enough to fill your deep fryer)

2 cups boiled peanuts (measured out of the shell)

½ onion, finely diced

1 jalapeño, finely diced (with or without seeds, your preference)

⅓ cup flour

2 tablespoons unsweetened peanut butter

2 cloves garlic, minced

2 tablespoons chopped cilantro

1 teaspoon Head Spice (page 16)

2 tablespoons crushed peanuts (for topping)

1 jalapeño, thinly sliced (for topping)

Make the Peanut Butter Molasses

In a medium-sized bowl, mix the ingredients together with a whisk.

Make the Falafel

Heat the oil to 350°F in a deep fryer or pot large enough to safely deep-fry.

In a food processor, blend the peanuts with the rest of the ingredients, using a pulsing motion so as to not beat the peanuts into a paste. This mixture should come together so that you can form a ball with your hands. If it is still pretty sticky, you can add a bit more flour.

Form the dough into approximately 12 (1-ounce) balls. Carefully drop each ball into the fryer and fry for 7 minutes, or until crispy and browned. Remove and place onto a wire rack. Drizzle with peanut molasses, chopped peanuts, and jalapeño.

FRIED CATFISH
WITH TOMATO SOFRITO AND FENNEL SLAW
Yield: 4 servings

Southerners' love of catfish probably began because it was regularly pulled up while fishing all over the region. However, it has continued as a menu staple in large part due to the abundance of catfish farms today. Catfish is an inexpensive fish, yet it still has a mild tasting, succulent white flesh. As for the rest of this recipe, while sofrito isn't a Southern sauce, its aromatic tomato goodness is amazing on top of the crispy fried catfish. To tie it all together, the slaw adds the perfect fresh crunch to this dish.

The sofrito takes a couple of hours, so start that first, then marinate the catfish. Once the sofrito is complete, the meal should be ready. We recommend serving this dish over a pile of grits. Sure, it's yet another thing to prepare—but you won't regret it.

Ingredients

FOR THE SOFRITO:

- 2 cups olive oil
- 1 onion, sliced
- 2 celery stalks, finely diced
- 8 cloves garlic, peeled
- ½ head fennel, tops removed and bulbs sliced (reserve the tops for garnish and the other half for the slaw)
- 1 teaspoon fennel seeds
- ½ cup dry white wine
- 1 (6-ounce) can tomato paste
- 1 tomato, diced
- 1 teaspoon chopped fresh oregano
- ¼ cup chopped country ham (optional)
- Salt and pepper to taste

Make the Sofrito

In a medium-sized stockpot, add the olive oil, onions, diced celery, garlic cloves, and fennel slices and seeds. Cook over medium-low heat for 45 minutes to 1 hour, or until the fennel and garlic are completely soft.

Whisk in the white wine and tomato paste. The tomato paste will take a little while to combine with the oil, but it will mix in well with a little whisking. Once the mixture is fully combined, add the diced tomato, oregano, and country ham. Season with salt and pepper to taste.

RECIPE CONTINUES

FOR THE FENNEL SLAW:

½ bulb fennel

    Zest and juice of 1 orange

1 tablespoon sugar

1 tablespoon chopped fresh basil

FOR THE FRIED CATFISH:

4 filets fresh catfish

2 cups buttermilk

1 tablespoon Head Spice (page 16)

½ cup vegetable oil for frying

2 cups Biscuit Head Dredge (page 94)

1 cup cornmeal

Make the Fennel Slaw

Finely chop the fennel or slice thin on a mandoline. Toss with all the other ingredients and put it into the refrigerator for about 1 hour.

Make the Catfish

Place the catfish in a shallow bowl suitable for marinating. Mix the buttermilk and the Head Spice together and pour over the catfish. Let the catfish marinate while the sofrito is cooking.

In a good-sized cast-iron skillet, add enough oil to cover the bottom of the pan and then add little more. Bring the oil to about 350°F.

Mix the cornmeal and dredge. Remove the catfish from the buttermilk marinade and coat very well with the dredge/cornmeal breading.

Very carefully lower each piece of catfish into the pan and fry it up. You are going to want to cook each side for about 3 minutes before flipping. Make sure the fish is golden brown before removing it from the pan and putting on the wire rack.

To finish the dish, top the catfish with large spoonful of sofrito and then a spoonful of slaw. As we mentioned, it's even better if you layer it up over some grits.

SMOKED BEEF BRISKET

Yield: 8 to 12 servings

Brisket is the perfect cut of meat for a long and dry cooking process (which is exactly what smoking is). That's because brisket is a tough piece of meat that needs a long cook time, allowing for the fat to break down and a good smoke ring to build inside the meat. You'll find the fat melts right into the meat as it cooks, which keeps the beef plenty moist. So let's smoke some meat and pile it high on a biscuit!

Method 1: Smoked Start to Finish

1 large beef brisket, about 8–10 pounds

1 cup Head Spice (page 16)

12 to 15 medium-sized dried and cured logs, such as hickory, oak, pecan, or mesquite

Note: Method 1 assumes you have at least a simple offset smoker to use. If you don't, see the note at right and Method 2 on page 110.

Remove the brisket from the fridge and coat it well with the Head Spice. You may want gloves for this step, because you're gonna get your hands dirty! Give the brisket a nice rubdown or massage when applying the spice blend; this ensures that all of the crevices and grooves get filled and will help to form a beautiful crust on your finished product.

Now, before we get to the smoking, let's get a few things out of the way. First things first: there are numerous books and websites devoted entirely to smoking, as well as a plethora of different types of equipment and gadgets. There are a lot of options, and we've seen people get great results with a variety of setups—everything from a smoker that costs thousands of dollars to smokers made from an old broken refrigerator or metal drum. On the pages that follow, we're assuming you have a minimal smoking setup: just a simple metal smoker with an offset smoke box. If you already know how to smoke or have your own smoker, by all means adapt our recipe to that!

Note: For those of you who don't have even a simple smoker, you can use a regular grill in combination with a smoker box—which is a metal box you use to burn wood chips in. If you are using this method, make sure that there is no direct heat on the brisket. In other words, keep the heat source—charcoal or propane—to one side and the meat on the other. This is important so that the brisket doesn't cook too fast and has a nice long time to absorb all the smoke. If you use this method, you will need to keep your grill at 250°F–300°F and you will need to continuously feed chips into the smoke box. You also may want to consider this modification along with the braised technique on page 110.

RECIPE CONTINUES

SMOKED BEEF BRISKET (CONTINUED)

OK, here we go. Using a mix of hickory and pecan wood logs, start a controlled fire inside of the smoke box. Let the logs begin to smolder and turn into coals. Letting the wood burn this much first will allow the wood to smoke, generating indirect and low heat to the meat, while keeping the meat in an enclosed environment. This allows the meat to cook slowly and also absorb all the rich flavors of the smoke. We usually put the meat on about 30 minutes after we start burning the logs, but just make sure that they're smoking and going pretty good before you add it. Continue to monitor your logs in your smoke box, adding new ones when necessary to maintain a steady stream of smoke and a fairly constant temperature of 250°F to 300°F degrees.

You can help control the moisture loss within the meat by adding an open can of beer or a pan of water somewhere between the heat source (the fire) and the meat. The placement will depend on what type of setup you are using.

Note: While you already have your smoker fired up, think about what else might be good with a little smoky flavor added. We love to smoke maple syrup and honey to add a really unique flavor to dishes! Simply place whatever you want to smoke in a metal pan or dish next to the meat.

Smoking a large brisket like this will take 8 to 10 hours (in general, when smoking you should plan on around 1 hour per pound), so make sure you will be able to tend to your fire for that length of time. You'll know it's done when it reaches an internal temperature of 165°F, or when you can pierce the brisket with a butter knife with little effort. At this point, remove the brisket from the smoker and place it on a sheet pan to rest for 30 to 45 minutes. The resting is so the meat is as tender and juicy as possible. Don't skip it!

Once it has rested, you can slice the meat to your desired thickness and serve. Refrigerate any leftovers for up to 1 week. We recommend serving this with our Bacon Slab and Bourbon Baked Beans (page 144), and the Strawberry Buffalo Sauce (page 81).

Method 2: Braised and Smoked

1 large beef brisket, about 8 to 10 pounds

1 cup Head Spice (page 16)

2 to 3 medium-sized dried and cured logs, such as hickory, oak, pecan, or mesquite

FOR THE STOCK:

1 gallon water

1 can beer (whatever you have on hand)

1 cup apple cider vinegar

3 tablespoons Head Spice

1 large sliced onion

4 cloves smashed garlic

For this easier method, you're going to cook your meat in a boiling mixture of highly seasoned liquid or stock first. This is a method that will still taste amazing, but it takes less time and is perfect for anyone who doesn't have a whole day to devote to smoking. You will end up without a crust on the outside, but you'll still have a beautiful, flavorful, and tender piece of meat.

Remove the brisket from the fridge and coat it well with the Head Spice. You will want to massage the spice in well for this method too, even though you won't be forming a crust. This will just help to ensure that you get nice coverage and maximum flavor from the meat.

In a large pot, combine the ingredients for the stock, cover it, and bring to a boil over medium-high heat. You can go ahead and add the brisket anytime before it comes to a boil. Once the liquid is boiling and the brisket is in the pot, set a timer for 2 hours. You'll want to boil the brisket, covered, for 2 to 3 hours, or until it's fork tender. However, you should start checking the brisket at 2 hours. Note that as it boils down, you will need to add more water to ensure that the meat stays submerged. Be careful when opening the lid to peek at it; the steam can leave a bad burn!

After the meat has braised, you can smoke it for an hour or so using your smoker or your grill with a smoke box for wood chips (see page 109).

DUCK CONFIT HASH

Yield: 4 servings

"Confit" means to salt and slow-cook in fat, and the French have been enjoying this method of preparation for many years. Duck or goose is traditionally used because of the easy utilization of the outer layer of fat on those animals. In the process, the fat is rendered off and then used in the confit. For our recipe, you can render your own fat by cutting it off the duck and into 1-inch cubes, then slowly simmering it in a cup of water for an hour. Once the water has all evaporated and you are left with just the fat, pour it through a fine-mesh strainer. Duck fat is amazingly flavorful, and there's a reason you'll see it on menus across the country. If you don't want to render the fat yourself, you can sometimes find duck fat for sale at higher-end grocery stores.

Ingredients

FOR THE CURE:

- 1 cup kosher salt
- ½ cup granulated sugar
- ¼ cup brown sugar
- 1 dried bay leaf, crushed
- 1 teaspoon whole black peppercorns
- 1 teaspoon whole coriander
- ¼ teaspoon cinnamon

FOR THE DUCK:

- 1 orange, cut into slices
- 4 duck leg and thigh portions
- 4 cups duck fat

FOR THE HASH:

- 1 pound red potatoes
- 3 tablespoons duck fat from your confit, divided
  Salt and pepper
- ½ sweet onion, julienned
- 1 cup pulled duck confit
- 2 cloves garlic, minced
  Leaves from 1 sprig of thyme
- 1 tablespoon chopped parsley
- 12 slices banana pepper pickles (optional)

RECIPE CONTINUES

Make the Duck

Place all ingredients for the cure in a large resealable plastic bag or plastic container and shake to mix. Take a casserole dish with a lid or a large plastic container with a tight-fitting lid and spread a layer of the cure inside. Place the duck quarters on top of this layer, and then pour the rest of the cure over top. Be sure to rub or massage the meat with the cure so that it's very well covered. Place the orange slices directly on top and refrigerate for 4 hours to cure.

Once the duck is cured, remove from the salt and sugar mix and rinse the meat with cold water to remove any excess cure. Pat the skin dry with a clean kitchen towel.

In a 12-inch cast-iron skillet over medium heat, warm about ½ cup of the rendered duck fat. Once the fat is hot, sear the duck quarters in the pan. You want to slowly brown the legs so that the fat has time to melt. Once they're browned, cover with the remaining duck fat. At this point, most of the meat, which is still on the bone, should be submerged in fat.

Cover the cast-iron skillet with aluminum foil and bring the temperature down to a low, slight simmer, about 180°F. Cook the duck for 3 hours or until the meat is pulling away from the bone.

Once the duck is cooked, remove it from the fat and cool. Pick the meat off of the bones and place in a storage container that can hold high heat, like a stone crock. Pour the fat over the duck meat and store in the fridge. It is important to make sure the meat is completely covered in fat, as this will seal and protect the meat for preservation. This old French method of cooking and storing can actually preserve the meat for up to 6 months!

Make the Hash

Preheat your oven to 375°F. Working on a sheet tray, coat the potatoes with 2 tablespoons duck fat, add salt and pepper, and then roast until slightly browned and fork tender, about 50 minutes. Remove from the oven, cool, and cut into bite-sized pieces.

In a medium-sized skillet, heat the remaining tablespoon of duck fat over medium-high heat and sauté the sweet onion in it. Caramelize slightly, then add the potatoes. Brown for a minute and then add the duck. Keep this mixture cooking to crisp the duck and potato, then add the garlic and herbs. Remove from the heat, top with pickled banana peppers, and get it while it's hot.

BACON OF THE DAY

Ah, bacon, the magical meat candy. At this point, enterprising people have put bacon in everything you can think of from ice cream and coffee to lip balm and dental floss. Yes, those things really do exist. At Biscuit Head we like to use bacon as much as the next guy, and we do put it in all kinds of different dishes. However, when we play with bacon it has to do with adding new flavors to it. If you stop in often, you'll find that our "Bacon of the Day" specials change constantly. We put all different kinds of glazes and toppings on it with flavors ranging from sweet to spicy (always aiming to complement the natural smoky saltiness of bacon). This has become such a favorite of our customers—some don't even read the flavor anymore before ordering it!

MAKIN' BACON

Bacon is simply pork belly that has been cured and smoked. This process acts as a natural preservative, which is why people have been enjoying bacon in this country for many years before refrigeration existed. Although it is extremely versatile, to us it screams (or sizzles and pops) breakfast. We like a nice thick-cut, hickory-smoked bacon the best. Wright and Benton's are a couple of our favorite brands, though if you're lucky enough to live in WNC (western North Carolina—yes, that's a thing) grab some nice thick-cut bacon from Hickory Nut Gap Farm.

You Will Need

5-pound slab pork belly

1 cup salt combined with 1 cup brown sugar

> Note: You can also add spices or herbs to this rub.

Smoker with offset smoke box or grill with smoke box (see page 109 for more)

How to make your own bacon in 5 easy steps (and impress all of your friends):

Step 1: Take a whole pork belly and rub with the salt and brown sugar cure. Don't skimp! Use your hands to really rub the belly and make sure you coat it thoroughly.

Step 2: Let the belly rest in the cure, covered and refrigerated, for 10 days. You can flip the belly over halfway through to make sure it still has a nice coating of cure.

Step 3: Remove the belly from the fridge and wash off the cure with water. Pat dry with a clean washcloth.

Step 4: Smoke the belly over indirect heat at 180°F for 4 hours using your awesome smoking skills from the brisket recipe (page 109).

Step 5: Slice the smoked pork belly into thin strips and finish as you would store-bought bacon.

S'MORES BACON

Yield: 4 to 6 servings

This bacon is the perfect combo of sweet, smoky, gooey, and crunchy. It's a fun addition to any Fourth of July brunch, but heck, we'd eat it every day if we could!

Ingredients

12 strips thick-cut bacon

½ cup semisweet chocolate chips (or whatever chocolate you like)

5 graham crackers, crushed

½ cup marshmallow fluff

Preheat your oven to 375°F, line a sheet pan with aluminum foil, lay the strips of bacon on it, and bake them until they're as crispy as you like.

While you're cooking the bacon, set up a double boiler and melt your chocolate. Once the bacon has cooled slightly, place the strips on your serving dish and drizzle with the chocolate.

Heat the ½ cup of fluff in microwave for 30 to 40 seconds, then drizzle the fluff on the bacon by letting it trail off the edge of a spoon. Sprinkle with graham cracker crumbs and you are ready to serve!

BLUEBERRY BLACK PEPPERCORN BACON

Yield: 4 to 6 servings

We love doing sweet and spicy flavors with our bacon. The flavors just combine so well with the smoky, salty crunch! In this recipe, the blueberry syrup provides a beautiful flavor with just enough black pepper bite to round it out.

Ingredients

- 1 pint blueberries
- 1 cup brown sugar
- 1 tablespoon coarsely cracked fresh black peppercorns
- 12 strips thick-cut bacon

In a medium saucepan, add blueberries, sugar, and black pepper. Cook over medium-high heat until the mixture comes to a boil and then boil for 6 minutes.

Preheat the oven to 325°F. Lay the bacon strips on a cookie sheet and then paint the blueberry-black peppercorn syrup over the bacon.

Cook for just over 20 minutes or until the bacon is starting to crisp. This is ready to serve immediately.

HABANERO-SORGHUM BACON

Yield: 4 to 6 servings

This bacon takes sweet and spicy to a whole new level with the fresh habanero. The sorghum syrup helps to balance out the heat, but this recipe is not for a spice novice. If the habaneros scare you, you can get rid of the seeds to cut down on the heat or substitute a less spicy pepper.

Ingredients

12 strips thick-cut bacon

2 habanero peppers, minced with the seeds

½ cup sorghum syrup

When you're cooking store-bought bacon at home, it's easiest (and cleanest) to do it in the oven. Preheat to 375°F, line a sheet pan with aluminum foil, lay your strips of bacon on it, and bake until done. In a microwavable bowl, heat the syrup and the peppers for 1 minute. Drizzle over the cooked bacon and serve.

BACON-WRAPPED PORK LOIN WITH SMOKED MAPLE SYRUP

Yield: 8 servings

This dish is a showstopper that your carnivorous friends and family will love. The bacon wrapped around the outside of the loin traps in all of the moisture and flavor, leaving you with an extremely tender and delicious cut of meat.

Ingredients

FOR THE RUB:

¼ cup whole-grain mustard

1 garlic clove, chopped

1 tablespoon chopped rosemary

3 tablespoons maple syrup

1 tablespoon cracked black peppercorns

1 teaspoon salt

FOR THE LOIN:

2 pounds pork loin

2 pounds bacon, thin cut

1 cup maple syrup

Note: Instead of baking, you can smoke this loin for a few hours at 300°F instead. If you are going to smoke the meat, make sure you have your smoker set up ready to go (see page 109) and place the loin right onto the grates. You can also smoke the maple syrup! Just put the cup of syrup in a metal pan and keep the syrup in the smoker for about 1 hour.

Preheat the oven to 350°F.

Mix all the ingredients in the rub together, then give the pork loin the best massage it has ever had, making sure to coat the whole piece of meat.

Take a nice big piece of parchment paper or aluminum foil and lay it on your counter. Shingle the bacon slices lengthwise over on each other, overlapping slightly, until you have formed a bacon blanket that is the length of your pork loin.

Set the loin in the center of your bacon blanket. Pull one piece from either side up and cover with the next piece from the opposite side as if you were weaving. Once the loin is completely covered with the bacon, place the bacon-wrapped pork loin onto a greased baking sheet.

Cook for 50 minutes or until the bacon is browned and the internal temperature is 140°F. Let this beautiful piece of meat rest for 15 minutes, drizzle your finished pork loin with the syrup, and enjoy.

CHAPTER 4

On the Side

For us, side dishes are as important as main dishes. Heck, oftentimes we end up working them in as integral parts of main dishes. Look no further than our biscuit sandwiches for an example. A lot of our sides end up being piled right on top of or inside said sandwiches along with a meat or veggie.

Still, every side in this chapter is also wonderful on its own. We have a huge variety of flavors and textures to choose from, ranging from cold and crisp Sriracha Coleslaw to a warm and comforting pot of Collards Callaloo. And of course we have our good old Southern grits! At the restaurants, some people opt to get all sides for their meal, and for them we offer a side plate of any three listed on the huge chalkboard. Feel free to try the same thing at home! Pick your favorite three from the pages that follow and match them for an eclectic brunch spread.

BISCUIT HEAD GRITS

Yield: 4 to 6 servings

Grits are a dish that everyone in the South grows up eating. Usually grits are corn-based, often simply made from dried and coarsely ground kernels. Grits can also be made from hominy, which is an old method of treating the kernels with a lye solution. This causes the kernels to soften and swell, releasing the outer husk and breaking it down, creating a more nutritionally complete grain. It is then dried and ground coarsely for grits or more finely ground to create masa. (Masa is the corn flour that is the backbone of many Latin American foods.)

When buying grits from the store, you will be faced with many choices. Yellow corn, white corn, stone-ground, quick, or instant. At the restaurant we use coarsely ground white corn grits, but we are not opposed to yellow grits. The coarser, or stone-ground, grits will require a longer cooking time, but in our opinion it is the key to a better bowl of grits.

Grits are boiled in liquid (typically water or milk) at a ratio of 4:1, liquid to grits. You always need to season the liquid first so the starch soaks up the seasoning in the beginning. At Biscuit Head, we also add some kind of fat, be it butter, cheese, cream, or olive oil. The basic method is simple, but just as with biscuits, grits are a blank canvas. Grits can be made from simple and plain to rich and decadent. They can be seasoned to taste savory, sweet, or spicy and eaten with any meal, depending on their preparation.

This is our favorite basic way to make grits and the way we serve them daily. The smoked goat cheese adds an intense and complex flavor that we love. But, as we said, use grits as a springboard for your own favorite flavors. Get inspired, and make a beautiful bowl!

RECIPE CONTINUES

Ingredients

½ gallon whole milk

1 tablespoon salt

½ tablespoon fresh
cracked pepper

8 tablespoons (1 stick) butter

2 cups stone-ground grits

In a medium-sized saucepan bring the milk, salt, pepper, and butter to a low boil. With a sturdy whisk, stir in the grits. Reduce the heat and stir for about 5 minutes, keeping the mixture at a low simmer.

Now you will cook between 30 minutes and an hour, stirring constantly. The exact cook time is up to your grits. At the beginning, you are going to need to stir more frequently, making sure to stir all the way to the bottom of the pot. Grits are like little pebbles, and they will sink to the bottom of the liquid.

As the starch from the grits releases itself in the liquid, it will start to help keep the grain granules suspended. Once this has happened, you can stir less frequently. However, if you do not stir grits well in the beginning, they will sink and cook at the bottom of the pot. This will result in a starchy catastrophe!

Once your grits reach the consistency you like, serve immediately. There are endless toppings and additions you can make to our basic grits recipe, from savory to sweet. A favorite at the restaurant is a scoop of our Hoop and Jalapeño Pimento Cheese (page 88), which melts right in and makes for a gooey and delicious breakfast. A traditional Southern topping is Red Eye Gravy (page 51). A little ladleful on top adds the perfect amount of salty, meaty goodness. You could also try catfish, shrimp, a poached egg—the list could go on and on, but you get the point. Once again, we encourage you to play with your food!

Leftovers? Make Crispy Grit Cakes

Like any restaurant—or any responsible home chef, for that matter—we love to use our leftovers to minimize waste. In addition to throwing less food away, sometimes you'll end up making your scraps taste better than the original dish!

To make grit cakes, you will need warm grits that you can pour into a plastic container to set up overnight. If you have a 1-quart container (like the ones "to go" soup comes in), use that. If not, another round container or cup will work just fine. Simply pour the warm grits in, put the container in the fridge, and chill for 12 hours. When the grits are completely chilled, you can pop them out of the container and they will hold their shape. Cut ½-inch slices, and you're ready to crisp them up.

Once chilled and cut, they can be pan-fried in oil in a nice hot pan, or you can brush them lightly with oil and bake them at 400°F until crisp and brown. These make a wonderful gluten-free side dish and can go with almost anything else you're serving.

Cold Smoke It

At Biscuit Head, we top our grits with smoked chèvre. Wait, how do you smoke cheese without melting it, you say? The key is cold smoking. You can cold smoke all sorts of things you want to flavor but not cook, like cheese, herbs, spices, fish, honey, fruit, and even grains. So, yes, you could smoke your grits and the cheese! We use this method often because it's simple and fast yet infuses a ton of flavor.

You Will Need

2 metal pie tins

   Note: Use older tins or ones you don't mind getting dirty.

   Handful of hickory wood chips (found in stores near the charcoal and grilling supplies)

   Aluminum foil

   Whatever food you want to smoke

Head outside with your metal pie tins. Inside the first pan, light a handful of hickory chips and let them burn for a minute or 2. You want to get the chips going pretty well to get maximum flavor.

Now you're going to extinguish the fire using the second pie tin. All you need to do is turn it upside-down and place it over the other pan, cutting off the oxygen supply to the fire. This puts out the fire and lets the wood chips smolder. As soon as there is no flame (this only takes a few seconds) place your food in the pan that was on top acting as a lid. Transfer the chips carefully to this pan, being sure to keep them off of the food you're smoking. Cover the food and chips as airtight as possible with aluminum foil and let it sit for about an hour.

Believe it or not, this low-temperature steep will infuse tons of flavor in your food without actually cooking it. Just be sure to get it covered quickly with the foil so as much of the smoke gets trapped as possible. If your food isn't smoky enough, try a second round of smoking, working a little quicker with the transfer and the foil covering now that you know the process.

COLLARDS CALLALOO

Yield: 6 servings

Southerners have been slow-cooking collards in fatback and with other meats for ages. This leafy green has been found throughout the world and fares particularly well in our climate. We bring some of the African and Caribbean influences by taking out the meat and preparing them callaloo style. Callaloo is a dish that we fell in love with on the islands of Trinidad and Tobago, but it originates in Africa. The recipes vary regionally, but the Caribbean style we like best is traditionally prepared with either taro or amaranth greens and coconut milk, among other things. We substitute the Southern favorite, collards, in our version, but you can use any dark leafy green you can find. Kale or mustard greens would work well.

Ingredients

- 2 bunches collards, cleaned and washed
- 1 onion, diced
- 1 sweet potato, sliced with the skin on
- 2 cups coconut milk
- ½ tablespoon minced garlic
- ½ tablespoon salt
- Pepper to taste
- ½ tablespoon curry powder
- 1 pinch ground allspice
- 1 pinch ground cinnamon
- 1 teaspoon red pepper flakes
- ½ cup brown sugar
- 1 ½ quarts water

Collards are notorious for having lots of dirt and grit, so wash 'em well! We wash ours twice. After you have the collards nice and clean, chop them into 2-inch squares. If you stack them up on each other you can slice them lengthwise and then come back and cut them the other direction.

Once you have the collards cleaned and cut, all the hard work is done! Add all of your ingredients to a large stockpot, give a quick stir, and cook over medium heat for 2 hours. Keep a lid on the pot, removing it only to stir every 15 minutes or so. If there is any kind of toughness to the greens after 2 hours, keep cooking and feel free to add more water as needed. The finished dish will be thick, tender, and creamy.

Note: Collards and most other greens have a rib that runs down the center. You can either remove this by cutting along either side of the rib or leave it in. We choose to leave it intact because it adds a little texture to the finished cooked greens. We will, however, trim the rib off at the bottom of the leaf. Anything below the leaf just gets too hard and stringy.

SRIRACHA COLESLAW

Yield: 8 servings

This is actually a fairly traditional mayonnaise-based coleslaw with just a hint of good old sriracha hot sauce. If you don't keep sriracha on hand already, you should fix that immediately! It has such a unique flavor from the fermented peppers it's made with, yet it doesn't pack too much of a punch heat-wise. This slaw complements anything fried.

Ingredients

6 cups shredded green cabbage

2 cups shredded red cabbage

1 cup shredded carrot

FOR THE DRESSING:

1 heaping cup mayonnaise (we use Duke's)

⅔ cup brown sugar

2 tablespoons sriracha
(can be adjusted to your spice preference)

¼ cup apple cider vinegar

1 tablespoon chopped fresh cilantro

1 tablespoon minced fresh ginger

1 teaspoon garlic, minced

1 teaspoon salt

Pepper to taste

Combine the green cabbage, red cabbage, and carrot in a large bowl and toss with your hands to combine. In a separate bowl or in a food processor, combine all of the ingredients for the dressing. Whisk or process to combine.

Pour the slaw dressing over the shredded veggies and mix everything together until the vegetables are evenly coated. Cover and refrigerate for at least 1 hour before serving so the flavors can fully incorporate.

THE WESTERS' WHITE BEAN SALAD

Yield: 6 servings

When you stop into Biscuit Head in Asheville, you very well may run into a Wester. A husband and wife team, Mike and Amy Wester, help things run smoothly for us on a day-to-day basis—their passion and positivity is part of the lifeblood of our restaurant. Anytime we have a function or party, we try to get Amy to bring her white bean salad. It is so fresh, healthy, and flavorful that it has become everyone's favorite side dish at potlucks.

Ingredients

- 2 cups broccoli florets
- 1 cup carrots (sliced lengthwise in half, then cut into ¼-inch half moons)
- 2 cups cooked white beans
- ½ red onion, diced
- ½ red bell pepper, diced
- 2 tablespoons chopped fresh basil

FOR THE DRESSING:

- ¼ cup olive oil
- Juice and zest of 1 lemon
- 1 tablespoon Dijon mustard
- 2 teaspoons honey
- 1 teaspoon hot sauce (Cholula, or your favorite hot sauce will work)
- 1 teaspoon kosher salt
- Pepper to taste

In a small pot, bring a quart of water to a boil. Blanch the broccoli and the carrots for about a minute or 2, then chill in the fridge until a bit cooler than room temperature.

Once the vegetables are cool, combine the chilled broccoli and carrots in a large bowl with the white beans, onions, peppers, and basil.

In a separate bowl, whisk together the dressing ingredients and then pour the dressing over the bean mixture. Mix well and let sit for at least 30 minutes in the fridge before serving—this will not only get the salad nice and cold, but it will also give it time for the flavors to fully incorporate.

BISCUIT HEAD
MAC 'N' CHEESE

Yield: 6 to 8 servings

This is a simple, rich, and creamy macaroni and cheese recipe—a crowd pleaser, for sure. You'll find there are a few additions that make our mac extra delicious: heavy whipping cream, bacon grease, sriracha, and, of course, a couple of leftover biscuits! If you want to make a vegetarian version of this dish, just substitute butter for the bacon grease. It will still be amazing.

Ingredients

½ pound elbow macaroni

¼ cup bacon grease (or butter)

6 tablespoons all-purpose flour

1 cup whole milk

1 cup heavy whipping cream

1 teaspoon salt, plus extra for the pasta water

½ teaspoon cracked black pepper

1 tablespoon sriracha sauce

2 ½ cups sharp Cheddar, shredded and divided

2 leftover biscuits, crumbled

Preheat your oven to 400°F and grease a large casserole pan.

Boil the elbow macaroni in salted water until al dente. Drain the pasta and set aside.

Heat a medium-sized stockpot or large skillet over medium heat and add the bacon grease or butter. Stir in the flour slowly. Let this roux cook for 1 minute while stirring with a whisk. Slowly add the whole milk to this mixture while continuing to stir. Once the milk is fully incorporated with the roux, stir in the cream. This is now a béchamel, or cream sauce!

Add the salt, pepper, and sriracha, then slowly stir in 2 cups of the shredded cheese, saving ½ cup of cheese for the topping.

When the sauce is smooth and all the cheese is melted, stir in your cooked pasta. Once everything is well mixed, pour the mac 'n' cheese into your casserole pan. Top with the crumbled biscuits and remaining ½ cup of shredded cheese and bake in the oven for 20 minutes, or until golden-brown and delicious!

On Pickling

While pickling may make you think of lacto-fermented pickles or sauerkraut, not all pickles are made that way. People have been using the simple method we use for our chow chow and our other pickles for thousands of years. Rather than relying on fermentation, all you need to do is submerge the vegetable (or fruit) in your pickling liquid. The liquid has to be very acidic, so typically it contains a lot of vinegar as well as salt, cinnamon, garlic, or other ingredients that are natural preservatives or have natural antibacterial properties. The goal is to end up with a liquid that bacteria can't live in—but to also create a mixture that will make the food you pickle even more delicious.

SOUTHERN CHOW CHOW

Yield: 2½ quarts

Chow chow is a vegetable relish that can be found in most pantries across the South and typically is made with cabbage, green tomatoes, and chayote squash. There are tons of variations, though, and you can add virtually any vegetable you want to chow chow. We use the relish-like condiment on everything from biscuits and gravy to hot dogs to macaroni and cheese. This is also a flavorful way to use up some of those leftover squash and tomatoes from your garden during the summer.

Ingredients

- 3 cups shredded green cabbage
- 2 cups shredded green tomatoes
- 1 cup shredded chayote squash (you may substitute yellow squash if your market doesn't have chayote)
- ½ cup shredded carrots
- ½ sweet onion, shredded
- 1 cup shredded red bell pepper
- 1 jalapeño, shredded
- ¼ cup salt
- 2 cups water

Note: To make it easy, use the shredder attachment on your food processor to shred all of the vegetables.

FOR THE PICKLING LIQUID:

1 ½ cups apple cider vinegar

- 1 clove garlic, chopped
- ½ cup sugar
- ½ teaspoon cracked black pepper
- ½ teaspoon mustard seed
- 1 dried bay leaf

Place the shredded vegetables in a large stockpot with the salt and water and bring to a boil. Let the mixture boil for 5 minutes then remove from the heat.

Pour the mixture through a strainer and press firmly to release all the liquid. Set the vegetables aside and get your pickling liquid ready.

Combine all of the ingredients in a large stockpot and bring to a boil. Add your vegetable mixture, give a quick stir, and remove from the heat. This relish is served cold and will keep in the refrigerator for several weeks. If you would like to can it, follow proper canning procedures (page 56). The chow chow will taste great and have lots of flavor as soon as it's done, but if you can it and allow it to sit and soak up the pickling juice even more, you will get a much more intense flavor.

BBQ PICKLED ONIONS

Yield: 3 cups

These onions are so good on almost any biscuit sandwich. The mixture of smoky, sweet, and spicy, along with the crunch of the onion, is a perfect complement to any meat. These pickles go especially well with the Smoked Beef Brisket (page 109) or scrambled eggs.

Ingredients

- ½ cup apple cider vinegar
- ½ cup brown sugar
- ½ teaspoon sriracha
- ½ teaspoon cracked black pepper
- ½ teaspoon kosher salt
- ½ teaspoon smoked paprika
- 2 cups sliced sweet onions

In a medium-sized pot over high heat, combine all ingredients except the onions. Stir and bring to a boil.

Once the mixture is at a boil, add the onions and stir while continuing to boil for a couple of minutes. Reduce the heat and simmer for 10 minutes. You want to cook the onions down and let them melt into the pickle juice, but also you want a little crunch to remain. Pour these into whatever storage container you like and cool in the fridge. They will last several weeks in the fridge.

Biscuit Head's Awesome Pickle Juice

We use this pickling liquid in the restaurant to make all sorts of pickled veggies to go on top of our Bloody Marys. The vinegar, sugar, water, and salt are the base of the recipe and all of the spices are just there to infuse extra flavor. Feel free to change the seasoning to suit your tastes!

- 2 cups white vinegar or apple cider vinegar
- 1 cup sugar
- 1 cup water
- 1 dried bay leaf

- 1 tablespoon kosher salt
- 1 tablespoon whole black peppercorns
- 1 tablespoon whole coriander
- 1 clove garlic, sliced

Bring this mixture to a boil, then put anything you want to pickle into it. Boil for 5 to 10 minutes, depending on what you're pickling. For peppers, asparagus, green beans, and other smaller and softer items, boil for less time, closer to 5 minutes. For sliced beets, cauliflower, whole cucumbers, and any other larger, harder foods, boil for closer to 10 minutes.

Anything cooked in this pickling liquid can be canned for later enjoyment or saved in the fridge for several weeks.

CORN PUDDING

Yield: 4 to 6 servings

There are many different variations of corn pudding up and down the East Coast, but this one in particular hits the spot for us. It's a rich and creamy soufflé-style casserole that's based on a recipe Carolyn's grandmother made for her when she was growing up. The basic recipe is amazing, but feel free to play around with it a bit. We've added bacon, cheese, jalapeños, and all kinds of other goodies to it and it's always turned out well. You might want to double or triple the recipe if you're hosting a larger dinner—everyone loves corn pudding and it disappears so quickly!

Ingredients

1 cup heavy cream

2 ½ tablespoons flour

2 eggs

1 teaspoon salt

⅛ teaspoon cracked black pepper

2 tablespoons sugar

2 cups fresh or frozen corn (sweet white is the best)

2 tablespoons butter, cut into cubes

Preheat your oven to 375°F and grease a medium-sized casserole dish. In a large mixing bowl, whisk together the cream and flour until there are no lumps. Add the eggs, salt, pepper, and sugar, beating until it's evenly mixed. Stir in the corn and then pour the mixture into your casserole dish. Top with the cubed butter pieces and bake for 1 hour or until it's golden brown and doesn't move much when jiggled. Serve hot.

OKRA HUSH PUPPIES

Yield: approximately 24 hush puppies (6 servings)

Fried okra and hush puppies are both popular side dishes in the South. This dish combines the two, giving you a nice hot crunchy exterior with a soft, flavorful center. Because of the addition of okra, you can pretend these are healthier than your average hush puppy too! They make an excellent side dish or late-night snack.

Ingredients

Oil for frying

4 cups okra, diced small
(if frozen, thaw and drain before using)

1 clove garlic, minced

¼ cup minced onion

1 tablespoon finely chopped parsley

1 cup buttermilk

1 egg

1 tablespoon sugar

1 teaspoon salt

½ teaspoon cracked black pepper

2 cups self-rising cornbread mix (any brand is fine)

Preheat a deep fryer or large pot of canola or vegetable oil to 350°F.

In a mixing bowl, toss the okra, garlic, onion, and parsley until evenly mixed. In a separate mixing bowl, whisk together the buttermilk, egg, and sugar. Add this mixture to the okra bowl and stir. Add the cornbread mix and stir until everything is fully combined.

Carefully scoop 1-ounce (about a tablespoon) spoonfuls directly into the fryer. You can try using a small ice cream scooper. Let the hush puppies fry for about 5 minutes, or until golden and cooked throughout. Place on a plate lined with paper towels to drain for a moment, and then serve immediately.

These little guys are really good on their own but will pair well with the Sriracha Honey Butter (page 68) or the Chile Garlic Honey (page 76).

BACON SLAB AND BOURBON BAKED BEANS

Yield: 8 servings

This is a hearty bean side dish that hits your palate with big, bold flavors and keeps your belly full. It starts with navy beans, cooked for hours with brown sugar, garlic, spices, and delicious bourbon. The flavor is further developed with bacon. We top the pot with a smoky sweet bacon slab, which also holds the beans in their liquid as they cook. Put a poached egg on top of these beans, serve them with a biscuit, and call it breakfast. Yum!

Ingredients

1 pound dry navy beans

Note: These need to be cleaned and soaked overnight. See recipe instructions (page 146) for more.

1 sweet onion, diced

2 tablespoons thinly sliced garlic

1 green bell pepper, diced

2 cups diced tomatoes

1 ½ cups brown sugar

4 cups chicken stock

¼ cup ketchup

2 tablespoons whole-grain mustard

1 tablespoon molasses

¼ cup bourbon

2 tablespoons D'Arbol Sauce (page 82; or your favorite)

1 tablespoon chopped oregano

1 tablespoon Head Spice (page 16)

2 dried bay leaves

1 pound slab bacon

Note: Slab bacon is the bacon side that has not yet been cut into strips. You can find this at your local butcher or specialty meat shop. You can substitute thick-cut bacon strips if you can't find the slab.

2 teaspoons fresh cracked black pepper

RECIPE CONTINUES

BACON SLAB AND BOURBON BAKED BEANS
(CONTINUED)

The night before you make these beans, pour the dry beans onto a baking sheet and sort through them to remove any funky-looking beans or debris. You should do this every time you cook beans that are dry. You wouldn't believe the rocks, pieces of stem, and other things that you find when you sort them out first!

Once they're sorted, pour the beans into a large bowl, cover with water, and soak overnight.

The next day, preheat your oven to 300°F. Pour out any remaining water from the soaking beans, give them a good rinse, and drain again. Place beans into a large casserole dish or a cast-iron Dutch oven. Add the onion, garlic, bell pepper, and diced tomatoes.

In a blender, combine the brown sugar, chicken stock, ketchup, mustard, molasses, bourbon, hot sauce, oregano, and Head Spice. Blend on low until the liquid mixture is combined.

Pour the mixture over the beans and add the 2 bay leaves. Stir everything together in the casserole dish and top with the bacon slab. Sprinkle the cracked pepper over the slab. Cover the top of the dish with a lid or with aluminum foil if you do not have a lid.

Put the casserole dish in the oven to bake. After 6 hours, take the dish from the oven and remove the lid or foil. Return the dish to the oven and cook uncovered for 1 more hour. This last hour without the top is going to create a browned crust around the pan and will give you an intense roasted flavor.

Remove the beans from the oven and let them stand for 10 minutes. They should have a slight bit of firmness to them but should also be cooked through.

Carefully remove the bacon slab with tongs and a spatula and place it on a cutting board. Chop up the slab with a sharp knife, making sure to leave large rustic chunks, and return the meat back to the dish. Stir the bacon into the beans, and the dish is ready to serve.

CHAPTER 5

Eggs

If you keep chickens, or have friends who do, you already know there's a difference between farm-fresh eggs from free-range chickens and the typical mass-produced egg. Chickens cared for the right way—and fed the right feed—produce eggs that have a rich dark-orange yolk rather than pale yellow. They will have strong shells and nice whites that can stand up on their own (rather than running out all over your pan!). These are differences you will be able to see right away, but you'll also find that taste and nutritional value are vastly better than their factory-farm counterpart.

There are only two ways to get really good eggs. The first is to have your own chickens. When you have your own hens, you're able to feed them whatever you want and can ensure that they're living a happy and healthy life. While raising chickens is not as hard as it seems and is extremely rewarding, it may not be a reality for you. In that case, we recommend going to the farmers market and buying them fresh from a local farmer. Once you've had the real deal, we guarantee you won't look back. They really are that much better.

Now that you know the type of eggs you need if you want to cook the best eggs possible, we'll go through a variety of ways to cook them. While some restaurants are adamant about one or the other, we cook all the dishes that follow both in pans and on a flattop. Both of them work well as long as you use the proper fat to prevent the eggs from sticking and keep them from getting too dark in color. Pan spray works OK, but our favorite thing to use is clarified butter. The reasons are, of course, that unique buttery flavor and the high smoke point. Regular butter can work in a pinch, but have you ever noticed when you put a pat of butter in a very hot pan that it turns brown and smokes? If you drop your eggs into this butter, they will get dark and they'll have more of a toasted flavor. That's because the milk solids in the butter, have started to burn. This will affect the flavor and look of the egg, and it can also cause the egg to stick to the pan, which you definitely don't want! Clarified butter is the solution to these problems. It is simply regular butter but with all the milk solids removed. You can make your own clarified butter and keep it for several months (see page 151), or look for ghee, an Indian style of clarified butter, at the store.

Clarified Butter

Ready to make the ultimate butter for cooking eggs? Let's clarify!

YOU WILL NEED

1 pound unsalted butter

1 medium-sized saucepan

Cheesecloth or a coffee filter

1 large Mason jar or other heatproof vessel to catch and store the hot butter

Melt the butter in the saucepan over low heat and continue to cook for 30 to 40 minutes. There is no need to stir, so just leave it be! The first time you do this, you should watch the butter the entire time though. You will notice the butter taking many different forms. First it will melt, then it will bubble, then steam, and finally a layer of white foam will rise to the top. The foam will continue to rise for a bit, but once it settles, the butter will start to be clear enough to see to the bottom of the pan.

Turn off the heat and pour the melted butter through cheesecloth, a coffee filter, or a mesh strainer into a Mason jar or another container that can handle high temperatures. When pouring, be sure to stop when you get to the milk solids that have sunk to the bottom. At this point you can keep the clarified butter out on the counter for a couple of weeks or store it for even longer in the fridge.

SUNNY-SIDE UP
AND OTHER FRIED EGGS

Sunny-side up eggs are simply fried eggs that have not been flipped. This keeps the yolk intact and very visible and makes for a runnier egg. We think these are the prettiest eggs and make a great addition on top of anything from biscuits and gravy to fried rice. So this is our all-purpose "put an egg on it" egg!

Over easy, over medium, and over hard are your most common other options for fried eggs. Over easy, also called fried light, is when the white is cooked through and the egg has been flipped but the yolks are still runny. Some people also refer to these as "dippy eggs," as they're runny enough to dip your toast or biscuits into them. Over medium, or fried medium, is an egg that has been flipped as well. Like over easy, a medium egg will also have the whites cooked through, but the yolks will be gooey instead of runny. Over hard, or fried hard, is an egg where the yolks have popped and the whites are really burnt to a crisp. While this might sound like a tragedy to the over-easy fans, these eggs are actually pretty good with cheese melted on top and served on a biscuit sandwich with avocado and bacon.

THE SUNNY SIDE

If you are looking for the picture-perfect circular sunny-side egg, use an 8-inch nonstick pan. If you are cooking on the griddle, that's OK too. Make sure to use enough butter to cover anywhere the eggs will touch, though.

Ingredients

2 eggs

1 teaspoon clarified butter (page 150)

Salt and pepper

Heat your pan on medium-low and add the clarified butter. Once the butter melts, drop your 2 eggs gently into the pan without breaking the yolks. Let them cook slowly for about 3 to 4 minutes. Once the white of the egg is cooked through, they are done.

Top with a little salt and pepper and serve immediately.

Note: Sometimes the whites of the egg are a little thicker near the yolk; if you poke them with a skewer or fork, being careful not to pop the yolk, you will help to decrease the cooking time and make sure that all the white cooks through.

FRY 'EM UP

Just as for sunny-side up, we recommend using an 8-inch nonstick frying pan if you have one. Set the pan over medium heat and add your clarified butter. Crack the eggs into the pan, being careful not to break the yolks. After you drop the eggs in the pan, poke the white next to the yolk with a skewer or fork. This will help the whites to cook more evenly.

Ingredients

2 eggs

1 teaspoon clarified butter (page 150)

Pan spray

Salt and pepper

Note: Don't be afraid to touch your food as you learn! Sometimes that is the best way to tell when things are done and the more you test the way things feel, the better you will be at figuring it out by sight in the future.

Once the white is nearly cooked through, it's time for the flip. Use pan spray on the top of the eggs before you flip. This keeps the eggs from sticking on the flipped side.

To flip the egg in the pan, make sure that the egg is loose by giving it a little swirl. Next, tilt the pan forward and away from yourself with a little wrist motion, tilt your wrist down and then flip it up while pulling your arm slightly towards yourself. This takes some practice and you may bust the first few yolks. (You can also practice this with a piece of toast until you get the hang of it. Good luck, y'all!) If you are cooking on a griddle, flip with a thin metal spatula that is large enough to support at least the diameter of the yolk—the white can bend and move around, but if the yolk bends over the edge of the spatula, it will break.

How to tell when the eggs are done: the easy egg is ready when the yolk has quite a bit of movement when you jiggle the pan or give it a gentle touch. The medium will look slightly firmer but still have a little movement with a jiggle of the pan. And the hard will look solid, with no movement and should feel firm to the touch.

PERFECTLY POACHED

While many know poached eggs thanks to eggs Benedict, those unfamiliar with this style of egg often confuse them for a dollop of sour cream or whipped cream! We love poached eggs and use these in the restaurant for the majority of our biscuit sandwiches. Once you get the technique down, you'll find they are easy to make. And because you cook them without the use of any fat, they are healthier than fried eggs as well.

Ingredients

- 2 to 12 eggs (as many as you want to poach)
- 1 gallon water
- 3 tablespoons white distilled vinegar

Bring the water and vinegar to a simmer in a heavy-bottomed, medium-sized stockpot. Adjust the heat so that you maintain an even simmer—not a boil! Before dropping the eggs into the water, give the water a little stir in a circular motion to create a swirl.

Crack the eggs and gently drop them in one by one. The closer to the water the eggs are when you drop them in, the more gently the splash will be and the shorter the egg white "tail" will be.

Cook the eggs for approximately 3 minutes for a light- to medium-done egg. If you like them harder, simmer for another minute or 2. Remove the eggs from the water with a slotted spoon. Obviously, the more eggs you have to cook, the more likely it is you'll want to work in batches to keep track of cooking time. If you're trying to poach a dozen eggs, by the time you crack the twelfth, the first egg will probably be done—and you'll be asking yourself, "Now which one was the first egg again?"

Poached eggs will hold their warmth for only 10 minutes, so it's best to serve them immediately. If you're hosting a large brunch, you can also make them ahead of time and transfer them from the poaching pot to an ice water bath. This will stop the cooking process and they can be reheated later in simmering water for about 1 minute. If you know you'll be reheating, go ahead and slightly undercook the eggs while they're poaching to prevent them from getting too hard when reheated. And remember, these eggs will need a pinch of salt right before you serve them.

HOLLANDAISE SAUCE

Yield: 2 cups

Once you have poached eggs, you're just a slice of country ham and hollandaise sauce away from making a Benedict (we're assuming you already have a biscuit ready, of course!). At Biscuit Head, we use hollandaise to top a variety of biscuit Benedicts: the brisket biscuit, our fried green tomato Benedict, and our Cajun Benedict.

You'll find this sauce is light and airy with a perfect balance of rich butteriness and a bright zing from the lemon and cayenne. While hollandaise can be an intimidating sauce for some people to attempt at home, if you follow the instructions, you'll be just fine!

Ingredients

8 tablespoons (1 stick) butter

4 egg yolks

2 tablespoons water

Juice of 1 lemon

Pinch of salt

Pinch of ground cayenne pepper

Pinch of black pepper

Pinch of smoked paprika

WHAT TO GET READY BEFORE YOU START

Very clean metal bowl with high sides

A double boiler (or a pot of water under a metal bowl, forming a double boiler)

A clean piano whisk

Note: There are two types of whisks, piano and French. Piano whisks are very thin and used to incorporate air into whatever you're stirring. The French whisks are much stiffer and are used to stir thick sauces such as gravy.

Melt the butter and set it aside somewhere warm.

Over a double boiler with water hot enough to create steam, vigorously whisk the egg yolks, water, lemon juice, and spices. This accomplishes two things. First we are cooking the eggs so they are safe to eat, but we are doing so in a way that is gentle and not scrambling them. Second, we are incorporating air into our eggs, which gives them volume and makes for a very light and airy sauce. The constant whisking of this sauce is what is so challenging. Stir, stir, and stir some more until the eggs are thick and the mixture is noticeably paler in color and has doubled in volume. It should take at least 5 to 10 minutes, depending on how hard you're whisking.

Once you're done whisking on the double boiler, take the mixture away from the heat and slowly whisk the melted butter into the egg mixture. You must be very careful to pour the butter in slowly so that the sauce does not break (or separate). A hand-held mixer could help with this task, especially if your arm is tired from whisking over the double boiler, but we always do it by hand.

Once all the butter is incorporated, you're done—and can finally rest your arm! The hollandaise should be served at room temperature within 4 hours of making it. This sauce can't be reheated because you will end up scrambling the egg, which is definitely not the desired texture.

SCRAMBLED, PLEASE!

Yield: 2 servings

The key to making the perfect scrambled eggs is to keep them moving in the pan. Scrambled eggs should be light, creamy, and fluffy, and never dry, hard, or browned.

Ingredients

- 1 teaspoon clarified butter
- 4 eggs, cracked and whisked in a bowl
- 1 tablespoon butter
- 1 tablespoon heavy cream
  (milk or half-and-half can be substituted)
- Salt and pepper

Note: Just before removing the eggs from the heat, you can stir in some sharp Cheddar for cheesy eggs or add a little D'Arbol Sauce (page 82) for some next-level scrambled eggs.

In a medium-sized nonstick pan over medium heat, add a little clarified butter and let it melt to coat the pan. Pour your beaten eggs into the preheated pan and stir ferociously with a rubber spatula. Be sure to keep these babies moving.

Once the eggs are starting to come together, add the butter, cream, and salt and pepper. Keep stirring until just about done. The eggs should look moist but not soggy. Turn off the heat and scrape onto your serving dish. The eggs will continue to cook a bit and will be perfect in a minute or 2.

QUINOA SCRAMBLE

Yield: 3 to 4 servings

This scramble is packed full of protein and will get you energized and ready for your day. We serve this at the restaurant and people love it as much as the "less healthy" dishes! You can substitute egg whites if you'd like.

Ingredients

1 tablespoon olive oil

½ cup sliced cremini mushrooms

1 teaspoon chopped garlic

¼ cup diced tomatoes

1 cup cooked quinoa

5 eggs, cracked and whisked in a bowl

¼ cup chopped kale, arugula, or spinach

1 tablespoon chopped fresh basil

Salt and pepper

Head Spice for seasoning (optional, page 16)

Note: Set aside some extra diced tomato and basil for garnish.

In a large nonstick pan over medium-high heat, add the oil and sauté the mushrooms, garlic, and tomatoes. These vegetables are going to release liquid, and you are going to stir them until most of the juices have evaporated.

Now add the quinoa and eggs and stir constantly as if you were making scrambled eggs. Once the eggs have almost cooked through, add the greens and basil, and season with salt and pepper or a little Head Spice.

Stir for 1 more minute and remove from the heat. Top with some diced tomatoes and basil.

OVEN-BAKED EGGS
WITH BISCUITS, GRAVY, AND CHOW CHOW

Yield: 6 servings

This is a great dish to make the day after you make biscuits and gravy. The biscuits don't have to be fresh for this one, so it's an ideal way to use your leftovers and make something fun and different. Of course, you can also make biscuits and gravy just for this dish if you want to.

Ingredients

1 tablespoon melted butter

3 leftover biscuits, crumbled into medium-sized pieces

1 ½ cups leftover gravy—any kind

6 large eggs

Salt and pepper

¼ cup shredded Cheddar cheese

1 quart hot water

Southern Chow Chow (page 139)

Note: For this dish you will need 6 individual 1-cup ramekins and your deepest baking pan or casserole dish that will fit all the ramekins inside.

Preheat your oven to 350°F. Brush the inside of the ramekins with melted butter. Fill the bottom of the ramekins with the crumbled biscuit. Heat the gravy in a saucepan or the microwave and pour over the biscuits in each ramekin. Add one egg to each ramekin—just crack the shell and pour the egg in. Season with salt and pepper and top each one with its fair share of the shredded Cheddar.

Place the ramekins in a baking pan or casserole dish and fill the pan with hot water until the water comes halfway up the side of the ramekins. This is called a water bath and will help regulate the temperature of the eggs so they cook evenly. Place the pan in the oven and bake for 15 to 20 minutes, or until the whites are done and the yolks are still a little runny. Carefully remove the pan from the oven—remember, it is filled with hot water! Remove the ramekins from the water bath. Just be careful, because the ramekins will now be very hot. Top each with a spoonful of chow chow and serve.

THE PERFECT QUICHE
WITH BISCUIT CRUST

Yield: 1 (10-inch) quiche

This is the base for our favorite weekend quiche. That said, we almost never serve it as you see here. We add all sorts of goodies depending on the season, from local mushrooms to fresh chard! Likewise, you should feel free to experiment with your own additions, not only to the filling but also to the crust. The important thing is that you don't add too much liquid beyond what the recipe calls for. So if you are adding mushrooms, spinach, or tomatoes—or other foods that have a high water content—they need to be cooked first so that some of the water can cook off before being added to the quiche. See page 166 for some ideas to get you started.

Ingredients

FOR THE BISCUIT CRUST:

2 ½ cups self-rising biscuit flour, such as White Lily

4 tablespoons butter, chilled and diced

1 cup whole buttermilk

1 tablespoon butter, melted

FOR THE QUICHE FILLING:

6 large eggs

3 cups half-and-half

1 ½ teaspoons salt

½ teaspoon cracked black pepper

Note: You will need a pie tin for this recipe.

Preheat your oven to 350°F. Make the biscuit crust as if you were making biscuits (page 26), stopping just before you would bake them. As always, be sure not to overmix your dough.

Coat the bottom of your quiche pan with a little melted butter, then spread the biscuit mix in evenly with a rubber spatula until you have a 1-inch layer. Place the pan in the oven and bake for 12 minutes or until it just starts to brown.

While the crust is cooking, crack the eggs into a blender and add the half-and-half as well as the salt and pepper. Once the crust is ready, remove it from the oven and reduce the temperature to 325°F. Pour the egg mixture into the crust, return it to the oven, and bake for 1 ½ hours or until the middle of the quiche is firm when you give it a shake.

Remove the quiche from the oven and let it cool for 15 to 20 minutes or until it sets up enough to cut. You can serve it hot or let it cool to serve cold the next day. It also heats up quite well in the microwave, but using the oven to reheat quiche will dry it out.

Quiche Ideas

Remember, this recipe is just the base for a quiche—the fun part is deciding what to put in it! In addition to the ideas that follow, we have one other piece of advice: don't be afraid to use your leftovers! At our house, a weekend quiche often is built from whatever we have in the fridge at the end of the week. We'll do a quick inventory of cheeses, meats, and veggies and grab whatever will taste good together. Experiment and you may find a winning combination all your own!

For these quiches, add the listed ingredients after you blend the egg mixture, unless otherwise noted.

Spinach, Bacon, and Swiss: ½ cup sautéed and drained spinach, 1 cup shredded Swiss cheese, 10 pieces of cooked bacon, chopped

Ham and Cheese: ½ cup chopped country ham, 2 cups shredded sharp Cheddar cheese (1 cup added to the crust and 1 cup to the egg mixture)

Veggie, Goat Cheese, and Herb: 1 cup cooked and drained mushrooms, ¾ cup goat cheese, 1 cup chopped fresh spinach, ½ cup drained roasted red peppers, and some of your favorite fresh herbs (thyme, rosemary, basil, whatever you like)

Roasted Tomato and Mozzarella: 3 sliced tomatoes, coated with olive oil and salt and roasted in the oven until liquid cooks off, and then chopped; 1 cup diced fresh mozzarella; 2 tablespoons chopped basil

Kimchi and Duck Confit: 1 cup chopped and drained kimchi, ¼ cup chopped scallions, 1 cup of duck confit (page 113)

KIMCHI AND BACON FRITTATA
WITH PICKLED SHRIMP SALAD

Yield: 8 servings

This is an unusual egg dish to serve for brunch or a late breakfast when you're hosting adventurous eaters. Don't be scared of the kimchi! It adds a wonderful brightness and spice to the eggs and makes for a delicious pairing. We serve this frittata with pickled shrimp salad tossed in a buttermilk dressing, so we're including that recipe here as well. However, you can certainly pair the frittata with more conventional brunch sides if you'd like.

Ingredients

FOR THE FRITTATA:

  6 strips bacon

  12 eggs

  4 ounces cream cheese, at
    room temperature

  ½ cup heavy whipping cream

  1 cup chopped kimchi
    (you can get this at most
    Asian markets)

  ½ cup chopped green onion

  ¼ teaspoon salt

  1 tablespoon olive oil,
    medium strength

Note: While the frittata is cooking, you can use your downtime to make the dressing for the shrimp salad (page 170).

Preheat your oven to 350°F and put a seasoned, medium-sized cast-iron skillet in the oven to warm up.

Cut the bacon into 1-inch pieces and fry in a sauté pan until crispy. Remove the bacon pieces from the grease and set aside. If you're making the shrimp salad, set aside the skillet, turn to page 170, and use the bacon grease to cook the shrimp.

For the frittata, you can move on to cracking the eggs into a large bowl and whisking them well. Cut cream cheese into ½-inch cubes and whisk into the egg mixture. Then add the heavy cream, kimchi, crispy bacon, chopped green onion, and salt. Mix well.

By this time the cast-iron skillet in the oven should be good and hot. Whip that cast-iron out, being very careful not to burn yourself. Pour in the tablespoon of olive oil and give it a little swirl in the pan. Add your egg mixture to the pan and place in the oven on the middle rack to cook for 20 to 30 minutes, or until the top is perfectly browned and the egg is cooked throughout.

To serve, put a slice of the frittata on each plate with a small mixed green salad topped with the pickled shrimp tossed in the buttermilk dressing.

RECIPE CONTINUES

KIMCHI AND BACON FRITTATA WITH
PICKLED SHRIMP SALAD (CONTINUED)

Ingredients

PICKLED SHRIMP SALAD:

12 large shrimp, peeled and deveined

1 garlic clove, sliced

1 teaspoon mustard seed

1 cup apple cider vinegar

1 cup water

Juice of 1 lemon (save the zest for the dressing!)

1 tablespoon light brown sugar

FOR THE DRESSING:

1 cup whole buttermilk

½ cup mayonnaise (we use Duke's)

1 teaspoon Tabasco sauce

¼ teaspoon chopped dill

Zest of 1 lemon

⅛ teaspoon salt

A couple turns freshly cracked black pepper

Reduce the heat on the pan you used for frying the bacon on page 169 to medium, and remove half of the bacon grease. Give the remaining bacon grease enough time to cool down. Add the shrimp to the pan and slowly sauté. Once the shrimp begins to turn pink, add the garlic and mustard seed, stir, then add the cider vinegar, water, lemon juice, and brown sugar. Stir until the sugar is dissolved. Pour the shrimp pickle into a shallow container and store uncovered in the fridge to cool. Let the shrimp sit in the pickling mixture until they are completely cooled, and then remove them to serve.

Take all the ingredients for the buttermilk dressing and place them in a blender. You don't need to blend for too long, just enough to bring it all together. Pour the dressing into a suitable container and refrigerate.

RED BEET DEVILED EGGS

Yield: 16 deviled eggs (from 8 whole eggs)

This recipe is one of Carolyn's favorites and pays tribute to her Pennsylvania Dutch roots. Red beet pickled eggs are widely available in grocery stores in Pennsylvania and were a staple in the fridge at her home. We love to take it a step further and devil the pickled eggs for parties. They are a showstopper thanks to the hot pink color and unique flavor.

Red Beet Pickled Eggs

- 3 large red beets (trimmed and cut in half)
- 6 cups water (or enough to cover the beets in the pot)
- 1 cup apple cider vinegar
- 1 cup brown sugar
- 1 teaspoon salt
- ½ teaspoon whole black peppercorns
- 2 bay leaves
- 1 ½ tablespoons spicy mustard
- 8 eggs, hard-boiled and peeled
- 1 onion, sliced

Trim both ends of your beets and boil in 6 cups water for about 20 minutes or until tender. Remove the beets from the liquid and set aside to cool.

Reduce the heat on the beet water to medium. Add the vinegar, sugar, salt, pepper, bay leaves and mustard to the water and cook over medium heat until the sugar is dissolved. Bring to a boil and remove the pot from the heat.

Place your peeled hard-boiled eggs and onions in a large bowl. Slip the skins off the cooked beets, slice them into large bite-sized pieces, and add to the bowl. Pour the warm beet juice and vinegar mixture over everything, cover, and cool in the fridge. The longer the eggs sit in the mixture, the more intense the flavor and color will be. We usually let them soak for about 24 hours, but this is up to you. Once they're done, strain the liquid off and place your eggs, beets, and onions in sealable containers. At this point you can eat the eggs the way they are, or take it to the next level and devil them.

From Pickled to Deviled

- 8 Red Beet Pickled Eggs
- ⅓ cup mayonnaise (we use Duke's)
- 1 tablespoon spicy mustard
- 1 tablespoon diced pickled onions
- Salt and pepper to taste
- 2 slices crispy cooked bacon, diced (optional)

Cut all your eggs in half lengthwise and carefully remove the yolks. Place the yolks, mayonnaise, and mustard in a food processor and run until nice and smooth. Stir in the onions, salt, pepper, and bacon by hand. Spoon or pipe the yolk mixture back into the eggs, and you're ready to serve!

Boiled Eggs

There are several ways to boil eggs, but we think this is the simplest way to achieve repeatable, perfect eggs. The only question is how do you like your boiled eggs? Just follow these steps and cook to your desired doneness. Note that if you're making deviled eggs, you'll want to cook them for 12 minutes, until the yolks are totally done.

To start, place however many eggs you'd like to cook in a medium-sized stockpot and cover the eggs by 1 inch with cold water. It's important to start with cold water so the eggs heat up slowly and don't crack. Set the burner to high heat and monitor the pot until it hits a nice rolling boil. At this point, you'll immediately remove the pot from the heat and cover it with a lid.

Set a timer now according to how set you want the yolks:
4 minutes for runny yolks
7 minutes for soft yolks
12 minutes done yolks

There are a few things you can do to get the shells to come off easily and not tear up the eggs once they're done. First of all, you actually want to use the oldest eggs you can find. The closer to the expiration date, the better, as the freshest eggs will be hardest to peel. Second, you can add a splash of vinegar to the water when you're boiling them and transfer your eggs to an ice bath when they're done cooking. Don't start peeling them until they are completely cool.

BLT EGG SALAD

Yield: 6 servings

Who doesn't love a good BLT? This takes all of those familiar flavors and ingredients and repurposes them into the perfect brunch or potluck dish. The individual little tomato bowls add a fun twist and make them easy to serve.

Ingredients

6 hard-boiled eggs, shells removed

¼ cup mayonnaise (we use Duke's)

1 tablespoon minced onion

1 tablespoon minced celery

1 tablespoon minced pickles

1 teaspoon pickle juice

½ teaspoon salt

   Freshly cracked black pepper, to taste

10 crispy cooked bacon strips, crumbled

3 large heirloom tomatoes

4 ounces arugula

Chop the eggs into a small dice and transfer them to a mixing bowl with the mayonnaise, onion, celery, pickles, pickle juice, salt, and pepper. Stir this together, folding in the crumbled bacon.

Cut the tomatoes in half, width-wise. With a spoon, remove and set aside the inside membranes of the tomatoes, leaving a tomato bowl. Set the tomato bowls aside. Pick through the tomato membranes and remove most of the liquid and some seeds; dice up the remaining flesh and stir it into the egg mixture.

Scoop the egg salad into the tomato bowls and garnish with bacon strips and some fresh arugula.

CHAPTER 6

★

Sweets

One of the best things about brunch is that you can have sweets for your main course and it's still acceptable to have dessert afterward. Let's hear it for sugar! Of course, we have all kinds of sweet jams and jellies and honeys, but that's for another chapter (see page 46). On these pages, we'll teach you how to make Biscuit Donut Holes and Biscuit French Toast. Or, for a proper dessert, maybe you'd rather try our Key Lime Pie in a Jar or the Buttermilk Ice Cream with Bourbon Figs. In short, if you enjoy sugar, cinnamon, chocolate, sorghum, or caramel, then this chapter's for you!

BISCUIT FRENCH TOAST

Yield: 4 to 6 servings

While you can use freshly made biscuits for this French toast, older biscuits will be drier and thus "thirstier" for the French toast dip. We've found that when the biscuits absorb more of the eggy mixture, they make for better French toast. (If you try to cheat and leave fresh biscuits in the mixture longer, they'll just get too soggy.) The other recipes here are optional, but they bring a lot to the table. If you are going to make the Sorghum Whipped Cream and Brown Sugar and Cinnamon Syrup (page 181), we recommend making them first. That way when the French toast is ready, you'll be ready to top it and eat right away!

Ingredients

4 biscuits (page 29 or 33)

4 eggs

1½ cups milk

3 tablespoons sugar

1 teaspoon ground cinnamon

4 tablespoons (½ stick) butter

Preheat a large nonstick pan or a griddle to medium (or 325°F). Slice the biscuits in half width-wise.

In a medium bowl, whisk together the eggs, milk, sugar, and cinnamon until combined. Dip the biscuit halves into the sweet egg mixture. Keep in mind that biscuits are more delicate than bread. You don't want to leave them in the egg mixture for long or they will get overly soggy. Put a slice of butter into the pan, let it melt, then place the egg-coated biscuits on the buttered pan and let them toast. Add a little more butter to the pan before flipping. We like to press our biscuit French toast with a bacon press, but you can use a spatula if you'd like.

After flipping, press the other side as well. The toast is done when the outside is medium to dark brown—or the level of doneness you desire. Use care when you flip them.

SORGHUM WHIPPED CREAM

Ingredients

1 cup heavy cream

2 tablespoons sugar

3 tablespoons sorghum syrup

Mix the heavy cream with the sugar and whip by hand or with a stand mixer until you have soft peaks. Slowly whip in the sorghum until combined, then continue to whip until you have stiff peaks.

Sweet as Sorghum

What's sorghum, you ask? Sorghum is an incredible grain that's been harvested for thousands of years. It's likely that the grain was brought to America on slave trade ships from Africa, where it originated. It adapted well to the regional climate in the South and it eventually caught on for its many uses. First and foremost, the highly nutritious grain is harvested to feed humans and animals alike. It can be cooked like rice or barley, ground up to make flour, and can be popped like popcorn. It can also be turned into ethanol and used as fuel. One of the most popular ways we use it today is by making a syrup or molasses out of the sugary stalk. We like it poured right over biscuits, pancakes, and French toast as well as in recipes like the whipped cream seen here and the Sorghum Seed Caramel "Corn" on page 199.

BROWN SUGAR AND CINNAMON SYRUP

Ingredients

1 cup light brown sugar

½ cup water

1 teaspoon ground cinnamon

1 tablespoon butter,
room temperature

Combine brown sugar, water, and cinnamon in a small saucepan and stir over medium heat until it just reaches a boil. Remove from heat and let cool for a minute; stir in the butter, and it's ready to serve.

BISCUIT DONUT HOLES
WITH LEMON CURD

At the restaurant, our take on donuts is a popular special. It's as simple as frying scoops of our regular dough, rolling them in cinnamon sugar, and smothering them in powdered sugar like a beignet. They're addictive on their own, served fresh from the fryer. We also like to serve them with a lemon curd. The next time you're making biscuits, give this a try with some of the dough!

Ingredients

Oil for deep-frying

½ cup granulated sugar

½ teaspoon cinnamon

2 cups biscuit dough (page 29 or 33)

Note: We recommend saving some dough when you make a batch of biscuits, or you can cut the biscuit recipe down and just make a small batch. If you save the dough, it will last for 24 hours in the fridge.

½ cup powdered sugar

Note: You will need a small metal ice cream scoop (#30) and a deep fryer or pot large enough to deep-fry. We recommend using a mild-flavored vegetable or canola oil for this recipe.

Set your deep fryer to 350°F or if deep-frying in a pot, start heating the oil. While keeping an eye on your oil temperature, you can shake the sugar and cinnamon together in a container with a lid or a plastic baggie to get them all mixed together. Place this mixture in a large bowl and set aside.

When your oil is preheated, dip a small ice cream scoop a little bit into the hot oil, which will help the biscuit dough release into the oil easily. Gently scoop the biscuit dough into the hot oil.

Work in batches, as overloading the fryer with dough can lower the temperature of the oil, and it can be hard to cook a large batch of donut holes perfectly. Fry for 5 to 6 minutes or until golden brown.

Carefully remove the donut holes from the oil and transfer them directly into the cinnamon-sugar bowl. Doing this while they're still hot will fuse the sugar mixture to the donut and make for a nice coating on the outside.

Place the donuts on a serving plate and coat with powdered sugar. The best way to do this is to put the powdered sugar into a mesh strainer or sifter and shake it over the donuts. This will give them a fine, even coating.

LEMON CURD

Yield: 2½ cups

This is a pretty simple recipe. The only matter of note for this one is to not use an aluminum pot to cook it in. The aluminum will react with the acid from the lemon and make your curd a greenish-grey color. Gross! Go for stainless steel instead.

Ingredients

- 1 cup sugar
- 8 tablespoons (1 stick) butter, cut into small pieces
- 4 egg yolks
- ⅔ cup fresh lemon juice
- Zest of 1 lemon, finely chopped

Put all the ingredients into a medium-sized saucepan. Before placing the pot on the stove, stir all the ingredients to combine. Note that they will not fully combine until the mixture heats up and the curd forms.

Low and slow is the safest and easiest way to make this sauce, so heat the mixture over low to medium heat, constantly stirring until it thickens. The curd will keep for over a week in the fridge, and is great on biscuits, toast, or muffins as well as the donut holes.

QUINOA PORRIDGE
WITH PECAN SUGAR

Yield: 6 servings

Don't let the word *porridge* scare you off; this is a deliciously sweet stewed breakfast that we serve at Biscuit Head in the cooler months. You can top this healthy and hearty porridge with any kind of nut, seed, or dried fruit you like. We like to top it with the pecan sugar mixture below and some fresh berries.

Ingredients

FOR THE PECAN SUGAR:

1 cup shelled pecans

½ cup granulated sugar

½ cup brown sugar

1 teaspoon ground cinnamon

FOR THE PORRIDGE:

4 cups whole milk

4 cups water

1 cup light brown sugar

1 teaspoon ground cinnamon

1 teaspoon vanilla

1 dash ground nutmeg

1 dash ground cloves

¼ teaspoon salt

½ cup steel-cut oats

1 ¼ cups quinoa

½ cup stone-ground grits

Make the Pecan Sugar

Blend all ingredients in a food processor or blender until finely chopped and well incorporated. That's it; you're done! Sprinkle as much as you'd like on top of your porridge and save the rest in your pantry to use later. This mixture will last for several months.

Make the Porridge

Add the milk and the water along with the brown sugar, cinnamon, vanilla, nutmeg, cloves, and salt to a large saucepan. Cook the liquid and spice mixture over medium heat until steam starts to rise from the pot when it's stirred.

Add the steel-cut oats and reduce the heat to a low simmer, leaving it uncovered. Cook for about 20 minutes, stirring every 5 minutes or so. After 20 minutes, add the quinoa and grits and continue to stir every few minutes until all the liquid is absorbed and the porridge is to a Goldilocks stage (as in "just right" for your taste). This will take about 20 to 30 minutes, depending on how thick you like your porridge.

CHOCOLATE BISCUIT BREAD PUDDING

Yield: 6 to 8 servings

Leftover biscuits are something you never want to trot out when hosting brunch, but we've found there are quite a few recipes that can elevate leftovers to the star of the show. This dessert and the Berry Biscuit Shortcake on page 190 are prime examples—they're not only welcome sweet additions to a brunch spread, but tasty desserts to serve after dinner as well. This bread pudding is wonderful with a spoonful of whipped cream, but you can also punch it up with some vanilla ice cream and our Chocolate Gravy (page 189).

Ingredients

4 large eggs

2 cups sugar

¾ cup coffee

½ cup cocoa powder

1 cup heavy cream

1 teaspoon vanilla extract

Pinch of ground cinnamon

6 biscuits, day-old
(page 29 or 33)

Preheat the oven to 350°F and grease a medium-sized casserole dish.

In a large bowl, whisk the eggs and sugar together until well combined. Stir in the rest of the ingredients except for the biscuits; this is your custard mix. In a separate bowl, crush and crumble the biscuits with your hands. Once you have the biscuits broken up, pour the custard mix over top and stir gently to combine. Pour the mixture into the greased casserole dish. Cover with aluminum foil and bake for 1 hour. To test doneness, insert a toothpick into the center or thickest part. If the toothpick comes out dry, then it's done baking. If there's batter on it, bake it longer.

CHOCOLATE GRAVY

Yield: 3 cups

This decadent sauce is made to be ladled under (or on top of) a slice of bread pudding! You can also pour it right over the top of a bowl of our Buttermilk Ice Cream (page 195) or use it as a sweet topping for a regular cathead biscuit (page 29).

Ingredients

3 tablespoons butter

3 tablespoons all-purpose flour

2 cups whole milk

1 cup sugar

¼ cup unsweetened cocoa powder

In a medium-sized saucepan over medium heat, melt the butter and slowly whisk in the flour, making a roux. Keep stirring over medium heat until the color of the roux starts to darken and becomes slightly golden. Slowly stir in the milk and keep whisking so that the milk and roux combine evenly. Stir in the sugar and the cocoa powder and keep whisking gently until the gravy thickens, about 5 to 7 minutes. Serve warm. Chocolate gravy can be refrigerated and reheated for later use, but it will be best the first time around!

BERRY BISCUIT SHORTCAKE

Yield: 4 to 6 servings

Leftover biscuits were practically made for this shortcake. Slightly dry biscuits are so ready to soak up the sweet bourbon berry sauce and the whipped cream. The result is a soft, spongy, and flavorful dessert perfect all summer long.

Ingredients

¼ cup bourbon

½ cup plus 2 tablespoons sugar, divided

¼ teaspoon vanilla

2 cups fresh berries

   Note: Any kind of berry is fine, so choose your favorites from whatever is in season.

1 cup heavy cream

3 tablespoons sorghum syrup

4 biscuits (page 29 or 33), cut in half or in thinner slices for layering

In a medium bowl, mix the bourbon with the ½ cup sugar and vanilla. Stir to incorporate. Toss the berries in this mixture and let them sit at room temperature for at least 1 hour. Stir every 10 minutes or so to make sure the berries are evenly coated and rotated from top to bottom.

Mix the heavy cream with the remaining 2 tablespoons of sugar and whip by hand or with a mixer until you have soft peaks. Slowly whip in the sorghum until combined, then continue to whip until you have stiff peaks.

To assemble this biscuit shortcake, top your split biscuits with berries and juice and a nice spoonful of the whipped cream. If you want to layer it up, simply slice your biscuits into thinner pieces and repeat!

KEY LIME PIE IN A JAR

Yield: 6 servings, 8-ounce jar each

We love key lime pie and we love putting stuff in jars, so for this recipe we did both! If you'd like, you can make it up to a few days ahead of time and just pop a lid on it. Then it's ready to go whenever you want to serve it—and everyone gets their own jar, which is fun. You can also top this pie with Raspberry Jam (page 61) or fresh strawberries.

Ingredients

- 4 egg yolks
- ½ cup plus 2 tablespoons key lime juice

  Note: Some stores carry fresh key limes and most grocery stores now sell key lime juice in the bakery aisle.

- 1 (14-ounce) can sweetened condensed milk
  Pinch of sea salt

Make a double boiler with a small pot of water heated to a slight simmer with a metal bowl over it. Add the yolks and the key lime juice to the bowl; whisk constantly, like you would for making hollandaise (page 158). However, for the pie, this isn't as much to incorporate air as it is to prevent the yolks from scrambling. Once the eggs get thick, stir in the condensed milk and salt. Set the mixture aside to cool.

GRAHAM CRACKER CRUST

Ingredients

- 2 cups graham cracker crumbs
- ¼ cup granulated sugar
- ½ cup brown sugar
- 1 pinch ground allspice
- 8 tablespoons (1 stick) butter

Preheat your oven to 350°F. Mix all ingredients, except for the butter, in a bowl. Melt the butter, pour over the graham cracker mix, and stir to combine. Pour the mixture out onto a cookie sheet and spread so that you have an even and thin layer. Bake in the oven for 10 minutes or until the crust starts to brown around the edges. Pull out the cookie sheet and let cool.

Assembly

Into each of the six jars, pour a little graham cracker mix. Tamp it down with the blunt handle end of a kitchen tool. Add some of the key lime mixture. For these layers, you can use a piping bag or a small ice cream scooper. Tap the jar so that the pie mixture settles and repeat until each jar is almost full. Screw on the lids and store in the fridge. Top with berries or jam when you're ready to serve.

BUTTERMILK ICE CREAM
WITH BOURBON FIGS

Yield: 2 quarts

When you make as many biscuits as we do at Biscuit Head, you go through a lot of buttermilk. There are many other uses for buttermilk besides biscuits though, and this ice cream is one of them. It is rich and tangy from the cultures in the buttermilk, which makes it interesting enough to stand on its own. However, it's also wonderful paired with desserts like the Chocolate Biscuit Bread Pudding (page 188) or with the Bourbon Figs (page 196).

Ingredients

2 cups heavy cream

1 cup sugar, divided

Pinch of salt

1 teaspoon vanilla

6 egg yolks

2 cups buttermilk

Juice and zest of 1 lemon

Note: The mixture you make in this recipe needs to go into an ice cream maker and spin until frozen. There are lots of different types of ice cream makers these days, but we just use the old-fashioned kind with lots of salt and ice. Just follow the instructions for your brand and you should have no problem with this recipe.

Bring the heavy cream, half the sugar, and all of the salt and vanilla to a simmer in a medium-sized saucepan over medium heat.

Meanwhile, in a separate bowl, whisk the egg yolks with the remaining half of the sugar until they are a bit paler in color. Once the cream mixture has reached a simmer, temper the eggs with some of the cream. This means you will add a small spoonful of the hot cream mixture to the eggs and stir. Repeat this a couple of times to ensure that your eggs gently come up to temperature and don't scramble.

Now you can pour the eggs back into the hot cream and stir. Reduce the temperature of the cream mixture slightly and stir slowly until the mixture starts to thicken. It is done when it coats the back of a spoon. Remove from the heat and stir in the cold buttermilk, lemon zest, and lemon juice. Cool the mixture for an hour or so and then transfer to your ice cream maker. Follow the manufacturer's instructions to finish the ice cream.

BOURBON FIGS

Yield: 4 cups

Figs are delicious on their own, but this recipe turns them into a gooey sweet treat with a nice toasty balance from the bourbon. Fresh or dried figs will both work well for this recipe, so use whichever you are able to get. They are a match made in heaven for the buttermilk ice cream, but they also make for a nice addition to a cheese plate.

Ingredients

Quart-sized Mason jar

Figs, dried or fresh, enough to fill jar

½ cup bourbon

1 cup water

2 cups sugar

Sterilize your quart Mason jar by submerging it in boiling water for a minute if you plan to can the figs. Remove from the water with tongs and place upside down to drain for a minute or 2. The container does not have to be dry to move on with the recipe. Pack the Mason jar with the whole figs.

In a small saucepan, bring the bourbon, water, and sugar to a boil. Carefully pour the mixture over the figs, leaving a little headroom. Screw the top on the jar.

Refrigerate the figs and use them within a week or so. If you'd like to can the figs instead, see page 56.

SORGHUM SEED CARAMEL "CORN"
WITH PEANUTS AND BACON

Yield: 6 cups

This recipe is a fun twist on caramel corn. Instead of the traditional popping corn kernels, we use sorghum seeds. You can find them online at wholesalers like www.nuts.com or at your local health food store. Just like corn, the sorghum seeds will pop open, and you'll find they're quite tasty. I mean, what isn't tasty covered in caramel and tossed with peanuts and bacon?

Ingredients

- 2 cups sorghum seeds
- 1 cup crispy bacon, chopped and set aside (save the rendered fat)
- 8 tablespoons (1 stick) butter
- 1 cup brown sugar
- ¼ cup sorghum syrup
- 1 teaspoon salt
- ½ teaspoon baking soda
- ½ teaspoon vanilla extract
- ½ cup roasted and salted peanuts, roughly chopped

Start by popping the sorghum seeds. We do this ½ cup at a time by putting them in a brown paper bag and folding the top closed. Use a bit of tape to seal the bag and prevent any spillage. Microwave for 2 ½ to 3 minutes, or until you hear them stop popping. Place the popped seeds in a large bowl and repeat until all the seeds are popped.

Preheat your oven to 280°F and grease a baking sheet with the reserved bacon fat.

Meanwhile, melt the butter in a large saucepan, then add the brown sugar, sorghum syrup, and salt; stir to combine. While stirring, increase the temperature until the mixture reaches a slight boil. Turn off the heat and add the baking soda and vanilla extract. Be very careful when adding the baking soda, as the mixture will temporarily double in size.

After you have thoroughly combined the mixture, add the bacon and peanuts. Pour the caramel mixture over the popped sorghum and mix completely with a wooden spoon. (Make sure you are using a wooden spoon because this caramel gets hot!) Pour the caramel and sorghum mixture onto the baking sheet coated in bacon fat and put into the oven for about 25 minutes or until it's deep, dark shade of caramel. Make sure you stir the mixture every 5 minutes or so and rotate the tray as needed so that it cooks evenly in your oven.

Once you pull your caramel corn out, transfer it onto a clean pan or surface lined with parchment paper and let it cool. Once it is cool, break it up and it's ready to eat!

BUTTERMILK PIE

Yield: one 10-inch pie

We are in love with this traditional Southern pie because of its silky custard filling and super-sweet tang. It may sound strange to those who have never had it, but just give it a chance. We think you'll fall in love too.

Ingredients

2 eggs

5 tablespoons melted butter

2 cups sugar

¼ cup all-purpose flour

1 ½ cups whole buttermilk

Juice and zest of ½ lemon

2 teaspoons vanilla

Pinch of nutmeg

1 10-inch pie crust, in a pie pan

Preheat the oven to 350°F. In a large mixing bowl, whip the eggs until they're slightly foamy. Stir in the butter, sugar, and flour; mix until smooth. Stir in the buttermilk, lemon, vanilla, and nutmeg. Pour this mixture into your pie crust, all the way to the top, and bake 45 minutes to 1 hour, or until it is browned on top and barely jiggles.

This pie needs to cool to room temperature or colder before being served. Leftovers can be saved in your fridge for up to a week.

ACKNOWLEDGMENTS

This book is dedicated to all of the lovely people who work at Biscuit Head; you guys are the butter in our biscuit. You are the heart and soul of the restaurant. Thank you.

Special thanks also goes out to all of our family and friends who helped us out on our journey. Whether you provided physical labor, love, support, money— or whether you were the one grocery shopping for us when we were too tired, or providing loving child care to our son, Cam—please know that you are greatly and deeply loved and appreciated. There is absolutely no way we could have ever created Biscuit Head, the restaurant or the book, without you all. Thank you for helping make our dream come true and for making it even better than we imagined.

INDEX

Page numbers in **bold** indicate photographs.

A

all-purpose flour, 13
Almond Butter, Marcona, 67
Amaretto Marmalade, 60
Apple Preserves, Honeycrisp, 61
Apricot White Ale Butter, 66

B

bacon
    about, 117
    Bacon Slab and Bourbon Baked Beans, 144, **145**, 146
    Bacon-Wrapped Pork Loin, 122, **122, 123**
    BLT Egg Salad, **174**, 175
    Blueberry Black Peppercorn Bacon, 120
    Habanero-Sorghum Bacon, 121
    Kimchi and Bacon Frittata with Pickled Shrimp Salad, **168**, 169–170
    making, 117
    S'mores Bacon, 118, **119**
    Sorghum Seed Caramel "Corn" with Peanuts and Bacon, **198**, 199
bacon fat, 17
Baked Beans, Bacon Slab and Bourbon, 144, **145**, 146
baking powder, 25
baking staples, 14
barley, whole-grain, 14
Basil Biscuit, Beet and, 38, 39, 40
BBQ Pickled Onions, 140
beans
    Bacon Slab and Bourbon Baked Beans, 144, **145**, 146
    dried, 14
    The Westers' White Bean Salad, **134**, 135
Beef Brisket, Smoked, **108**, 109–110, 111
Beer City Biscuit, **44**, 45

beets
    Beet and Basil Biscuit, 38, **39**, 40
    Red Beet Deviled Eggs, 172, **173**
Berry Biscuit Shortcake, 190, **191**
biscotti, 23
Biscuit Bread Pudding, Chocolate, 188, **189**
Biscuit Crust, 166
Biscuit Donut Holes with Lemon Curd, 182, **183**
Biscuit French Toast, 178, **179, 180**
Biscuit Head Dredge, 94
Biscuit Head Grits, 126, **127**, 128
Biscuit Head Mac 'n' Cheese, 136, **137**
Biscuit Head's Awesome Pickle Juice, 140
biscuits
    about, 19–20, 23–24
    Beer City Biscuit, 45
    Beet and Basil Biscuit, 38, **39**, 40
    Classic Cathead Biscuit, 29–30
    deconstructing, 24–25
    Gluten-Free Cathead Biscuit, **32**, 33
    Mac 'n' Cheese Biscuit, **36**, 37
    making, 26–27
    Roasted Corn and Jalapeño Biscuit, 41–42, **43**
    Rye Biscuit, 34, **35**
Black Peppercorn Bacon, Blueberry, 120
BLT Egg Salad, **174**, 175
blueberries
    Blueberry Black Peppercorn Bacon, 120
    Blueberry Jalapeño Hot Sauce, 80
Boiled Eggs, 173
Boiled Peanut Falafel, **100**, 101–102
Bourbon Baked Beans, Bacon Slab and, 144, **145**, 146
Bourbon Figs, 196, **197**
Bread Pudding, Chocolate Biscuit, 188, **189**
Brisket, Smoked Beef, **108**, 109–110, **111**

broccoli, The Westers' White Bean Salad, **134**, 135
brown sugar
    about, 14
    Brown Sugar and Cinnamon Syrup, 181
Buffalo Sauce, Strawberry, 81
butter
    about, 25, 26
    clarified, 150–151
    compound, 64, 66, 67, 68, **69**, 71
    for cooking eggs, 150
buttermilk
    about, 25
    Buttermilk Ice Cream, **194**, 195
    Buttermilk Pie, 200, **201**

C

cabbage
    Southern Chow Chow, **138**, 139
    Sriracha Coleslaw, 132, **133**
cake flour, 13, 25
canning, 54, 56
caraway seeds, Rye Biscuit, 34, **35**
Catfish, Fried, **104**, 105–106, **107**
Chai Butter, Sweet Potato, 62
Cherry Jam, Spiced, **58**, 59
Chèvre Dressing, 96
Chicken, Mimosa Fried, **92**, 93–94, 95
Chicken Fried Tofu, 98, **99**
Chile Garlic Honey, 76, **77**
chiles, D'Arbol Sauce, 82
chocolate
    Chocolate Biscuit Bread Pudding, 188, **189**
    Chocolate Gravy, 189
Cinnamon Syrup, Brown Sugar and, 181
clarified butter, 150–151
Classic Cathead Biscuit, 29–30
Classic Pimento Cheese, 90
Coconut Gravy, Sweet Potato, 53
cold smoking, 129

Coleslaw, Sriracha, 132, **133**
Collards Callaloo, **130**, 131
compound butters
    about, 64
    Apricot White Ale Butter, 66
    Marcona Almond Butter, 67
    Raspberry Truffle Butter, 71
    Sriracha Honey Butter, 68, **69**
cook times, 27
corn
    Corn Pudding, 141, **141**
    Roasted Corn and Jalapeño Biscuit,
        41–42, **43**
cornmeal, 13
Crispy Grit Cakes, 128
cutting in butter, 26

D

D'Arbol Sauce, 82
Deviled Eggs, Red Beet, 172, **173**
diced pimentos, 17
Donut Holes with Lemon Curd, Biscuit,
    182, **183**
dressings
    Chèvre Dressing, 96
    for Pickled Shrimp Salad, 170
    for The Westers' White Bean Salad,
        135
dried beans, 14
drop biscuits, 23
Duck Confit Hash, **112**, 113–114
Duke's mayonnaise, 17

E

eggs
    about, 149–150
    BLT Egg Salad, **174**, 175
    Boiled, 173
    fried, 153–154, 155, **155**
    Kimchi and Bacon Frittata with
        Pickled Shrimp Salad, 170
    Oven-Baked Eggs, 164, **164**, 165
    The Perfect Quiche, 166, 167, **167**
    Perfectly Poached, **156**, 157
    Quinoa Scramble, 162, 163, **163**
    Red Beet Deviled Eggs, 172,
        173, **173**
    Red Beet Pickled Eggs, 172
    Scrambled, Please!, 161
    Sunny-Side Up, 152, **152**, 153–154

F

Falafel, Boiled Peanut, **100**, 101–102
fat, 25
Fennel Slaw, 106
Figs, Bourbon, 196, **197**
flours, 13, 25, 26
freezer-plate method, 59
French Toast, Biscuit, 178, **179**, 180
Fried Catfish, **104**, 105–106, **107**
Fried Chicken, Mimosa, **92**, 93–94, **95**
Fried Tofu, Chicken, 98, **99**
Frittata with Pickled Shrimp Salad,
    Kimchi and Bacon, **168**, 169–170
fruit butter
    about, 54
    Sweet Potato Chai Butter, 62
frying, 94
frying oils, 17

G

Garlic Honey, Chile, 76, **77**
Gluten-Free Cathead Biscuit, **32**, 33
gluten-free flour mix, 13
Graham Cracker Crust, 192, **193**
grains, 13
gravies
    about, 48
    Chocolate Gravy, 190
    Crispy Grit Cakes, 128
    Pork Sausage Gravy, 52
    Red Eye Gravy, 51
    Sweet Potato Coconut Gravy, 53
grits
    about, 13
    Biscuit Head Grits, 126, **127**, 128

H

Habanero-Sorghum Bacon, 121
ham, Red Eye Gravy, 51
Hash, Duck Confit, 112, 113–114
Head Spice, 16
Herb-Infused Orange Honey, 73, 74
Hollandaise Sauce, 158, **159**
honey
    about, 14
    Chile Garlic Honey, 76, 77
    Herb-Infused Orange Honey, **73**, 74
    infused, 72
    Roasted Honey with Thyme, 75
    Sriracha Honey Butter, 68, **69**
Honeycrisp Apple Preserves, 63
Hoop and Jalapeño Pimento Cheese,
    87, 88, **89**
hot sauces
    about, 78
    Blueberry Jalapeño Hot Sauce, 80
    D'Arbol Sauce, 82
    as staple, 17
    Strawberry Buffalo Sauce, 81
Hush Puppies, Okra, **142**, 143

I

Ice Cream, Buttermilk, **194**, 195
ice cream scoops, 27
infused honeys
    about, 72
    Chile Garlic Honey, 76, **77**
    Herb-Infused Orange Honey, **73**, 74
    Roasted Honey with Thyme, 75

J

jalapeños
    Blueberry Jalapeño Hot Sauce, 80
    Roasted Corn and Jalapeño Biscuit,
        41–42, **43**
jam
    about, 54
    Raspberry Jam, 61
    Spiced Cherry Jam, **58**, 59

jam bar, 54

jelly, 54

K

Key Lime Pie in a Jar, 192, **193**

Kimchi and Bacon Frittata with Pickled Shrimp Salad, **168,** 169–170

L

lard, 25

leavening agents, 25

legumes, 13

Lemon Curd, 185

M

Mac 'n' Cheese Biscuit, **36,** 37

Mac 'n' Cheese, Biscuit Head, 136, 137

maple syrup

    about, 14

    Smoked Maple Syrup, 122

Marcona Almond Butter, 67

margarine, 25

marmalade

    about, 54

    Amaretto Marmalade, 60

mayonnaise, Duke's, 17

milk, 25

Mimosa Fried Chicken, **92,** 93–94, **95**

molasses

    about, 14

    Peanut Butter Molasses, 102

mustard, whole-grain, 17

N

nuts, 14

O

oats, steel-cut, 13

oils, frying, 17

Okra Hush Puppies, **142,** 143

Onions, BBQ Pickled, 140

Orange Honey, Herb-Infused, 74

oranges, Amaretto Marmalade, 60

Oven-Baked Eggs with Biscuits, Gravy, and Chow Chow, **164,** 165

overmixing, 27

P

pairing ideas

    Beer City Biscuit, 45

    Beet and Basil Biscuit, 40

    Classic Cathead Biscuit, 30

    Gluten-Free Cathead Biscuit, **32,** 33

    Mac 'n' Cheese Biscuit, **36,** 37

    Roasted Corn and Jalapeño Biscuit, 42

    Rye Biscuit, 34, **35**

pantry must-haves, 13–14, 16–17

Peanut Butter Molasses, 102

peanuts

    Boiled Peanut Falafel, **100,** 101–102

    Sorghum Seed Caramel "Corn" with Peanuts and Bacon, **198,** 199

Peppercorn Bacon, Blueberry Black, 120

Perfect Quiche, The, 166, **167**

Perfectly Poached eggs, **156,** 157

Pickled Eggs, Red Beet, 172, **173**

Pickled Shrimp Salad, Kimchi and Bacon Frittata with, 168, 169–170

pickles, 17

pickling

    about, 138

    BBQ Pickled Onions, 140

    liquid for, 139

Pie, Buttermilk, 200, **201**

Pie Spice, 16

pimento cheese

    about, 86

    Classic Pimento Cheese, 90

    Hoop and Jalapeño Pimento Cheese, **87,** 88, 89

    Smokehouse Pimento Cheese, 91

pimentos, 17

Pork Loin, Bacon-Wrapped, 122, **122, 123**

Pork Sausage Gravy, 52

Porridge with Pecan Sugar, Quinoa, 186, **187**

powdered sugar, 14

preserves

    about, 54

    Honeycrisp Apple Preserves, 63

Q

quiche

    ideas for, 167

    The Perfect Quiche, 166, **167**

quinoa

    about, 14

    Quinoa Porridge with Pecan Sugar, 186, **187**

    Quinoa Scramble, 162, **163**

R

raspberries

    Raspberry Jam, 61

    Raspberry Truffle Butter, 71

Red Beet Deviled Eggs, 172, **173**

Red Eye Gravy, 51

Roasted Corn and Jalapeño Biscuit, 41–42, **43**

Roasted Honey with Thyme, 75

Rye Biscuit, 34, **35**

S

salad

    BLT Egg Salad, **174,** 175

    Pickled Shrimp Salad, 170

    The Westers' White Bean Salad, **134,** 135

sauces, Hollandaise Sauce, 158, **159**

Sausage Gravy, Pork, 52

scones, 23

Scrambled, Please!, 161

seasonings, 16

seeds, 13

Shortcake, Berry Biscuit, 190

Shrimp Salad, Kimchi and Bacon Frittata with Pickled, **168,** 169–170

side dishes

    about, 125

    Bacon Slab and Bourbon Baked Beans, 144, **145,** 146

    BBQ Pickled Onions, 140

    Biscuit Head Grits, 126, **127,** 128

    Biscuit Head Mac 'n' Cheese, 136, **137**

    Collards Callaloo, **130,** 131

    Corn Pudding, 141, **141**

    Okra Hush Puppies, **142,** 143

Southern Chow Chow, **138,** 139

Sriracha Coleslaw, 132, **133**

The Westers' White Bean Salad, **134,** 135

sifting, 26

Slaw, Fennel, 106

Smoked Beef Brisket, **108,** 109–110, 111

Smoked Maple Syrup, 122

Smokehouse Pimento Cheese, 91

S'mores Bacon, 118, **119**

snapping, 26

Sofrito, Tomato, **104,** 105

sorghum

    about, 181

    Habanero-Sorghum Bacon, 121

    seeds, 14

    Sorghum Seed Caramel "Corn" with Peanuts and Bacon, **198,** 199

    Sorghum Whipped Cream, 181

syrup, 14

Southern Chow Chow, **138,** 139, **164,** 165

Southern Fried Green Tomatoes, **96,** 97

Spiced Cherry Jam, **58,** 59

spices, 16

squash, Southern Chow Chow, **138,** 139

sriracha

    Sriracha Coleslaw, 132, **133**

    Sriracha Honey Butter, 68, **69**

staples, 13–14, 16–17

steel-cut oats, 13

Strawberry Buffalo Sauce, 81

sugar

    about, 14

    Pecan, 186

Sunny-Side Up eggs, **152,** 153–154

sweet potatoes

    Sweet Potato Chai Butter, 62

    Sweet Potato Coconut Gravy, 53

sweeteners, 14

sweets

    about, 177

    Berry Biscuit Shortcake, 190

    Biscuit Donut Holes, 182, **183**

    Biscuit French Toast, 178, **179, 180**

    Brown Sugar and Cinnamon Syrup, 181

    Buttermilk Ice Cream, **194,** 195

    Buttermilk Pie, 200, **201**

    Chocolate Biscuit Bread Pudding, 188, **189**

    Chocolate Gravy, 189

    Key Lime Pie in a Jar, 192, **193**

    Lemon Curd, 185

    Quinoa Porridge with Pecan Sugar, 186, **187**

    Sorghum Seed Caramel "Corn" with Peanuts and Bacon, **198,** 199

    Sorghum Whipped Cream, 181

T

Thyme, Roasted Honey with, 75

Tofu, Chicken Fried, 98, **99**

tomatoes

    Southern Chow Chow, **138,** 139

    Southern Fried Green Tomatoes, **96,** 97

    Tomato Sofrito, **104,** 105

Truffle Butter, Raspberry, 71

W

Westers' White Bean Salad, The, **134,** 135

Whipped Cream, Sorghum, 181

White Ale Butter, Apricot, 66

White Bean Salad, The Westers', **134,** 135

white sugar, 14

whole-grain barley, 14

whole-grain mustard, 17

ABOUT THE AUTHORS

Husband and wife team Jason and Carolyn Roy opened the original Biscuit Head restaurant in Asheville, North Carolina, to share their love of southern cooking, their inspiration from travel, and their commitment to local foods. The restaurant has been packed since day one and widely featured in the media including the *New York Times*, *Food & Wine*, *USA Today*, *Garden & Gun*, *Paste*, and Eater.com. The Roys opened the second location of Biscuit Head, also in Asheville, in 2014 and their first South Carolina location, in Greenville, in 2016. All Biscuit Head locations strive to have as light of a carbon footprint as possible and participate in local charitable events. Find them online at: www.biscuitheads.com.